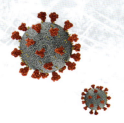

FIGHTING COVID-19 ABROAD

BY SUSAN E. HAMEN

CONTENT CONSULTANT

Judd L. Walson, MD, MPH
Vice Chair, Department of Global Health
Professor, Departments of Global Health, Medicine
(Infectious Disease), Pediatrics and Epidemiology
University of Washington

Essential Library

An Imprint of Abdo Publishing
abdobooks.com

ABDOBOOKS.COM

Published by Abdo Publishing, a division of ABDO, PO Box 398166, Minneapolis, Minnesota 55439. Copyright © 2023 by Abdo Consulting Group, Inc. International copyrights reserved in all countries. No part of this book may be reproduced in any form without written permission from the publisher. Essential Library™ is a trademark and logo of Abdo Publishing.

Printed in the United States of America, North Mankato, Minnesota.
052022
092022

Cover Photo: SeongJoon Cho/Bloomberg/Getty Images
Interior Photos: Paolo Bona/Shutterstock Images, 4; Francesco Giase/RVM Broadcast/Mondadori Portfolio/Getty Images, 9; Claudio Furlan/LaPresse/AP Images, 10; Babich Alexander/Shutterstock Images, 16; Shutterstock Images, 18; Dake Kang/AP Images, 20; Ren Yong/Imagine China/AP Images, 23; Chiang Ying-ying/AP Images, 28; I-Hwa Cheng/Bloomberg/Getty Images, 31; Debajyoti Chakraborty/Nur Photo/AP Images, 34; Alastair Grant/Pool/AP Images, 38; David Gray/Getty Images News/Getty Images, 44; Mark Baker/AP Images, 46, 49; Paul Zinken/Picture Alliance/Getty Images, 52; Dave Rushen/SOPA Images/Sipa USA/AP Images, 59; Andres Kudacki/AP Images, 61; Jerome Delay/AP Images, 64; Amos Gumulira/AFP/Getty Images, 70; Joseph Mizere/Xinhua News Agency/Getty Images, 72; Anna Szilagyi/AP Images, 76; Silvia Izquierdo/AP Images, 79; Natacha Pisarenko/AP Images, 82; Christian Palma/AP Images, 86; Aphotografia/Getty Images Sport/Getty Images, 89; Jonathan Hayward/The Canadian Press/AP Images, 95; Paul Chiasson/The Canadian Press/AP Images, 97; Red Line Editorial, 98

Editor: Marie Pearson
Designer: Becky Daum

Library of Congress Control Number: 2021951420
Publisher's Cataloging-in-Publication Data
Names: Hamen, Susan E., author.
Title: Fighting covid-19 abroad / by Susan E. Hamen
Description: Minneapolis, Minnesota: Abdo Publishing, 2023 | Series: Fighting covid-19 | Includes online resources and index.
Identifiers: ISBN 9781532197963 (lib. bdg.) | ISBN 9781098271619 (ebook)
Subjects: LCSH: COVID-19 (Disease)--Juvenile literature. | World health--Juvenile literature. | Communicable diseases--Vaccination--Juvenile literature. | Communicable diseases--Prevention--Juvenile literature. | Civilization, Modern--21st century--Juvenile literature.
Classification: DDC 614.592--dc23

CONTENTS

CHAPTER ONE
ITALY
4

CHAPTER TWO
CHINA
18

CHAPTER THREE
ASIA
28

CHAPTER FOUR
AUSTRALIA AND NEW ZEALAND
38

CHAPTER FIVE
EUROPE
52

CHAPTER SIX
AFRICA
64

CHAPTER SEVEN
SOUTH AMERICA
76

CHAPTER EIGHT
NORTH AMERICA
86

ESSENTIAL FACTS	100
GLOSSARY	102
ADDITIONAL RESOURCES	104
SOURCE NOTES	106
INDEX	110
ABOUT THE AUTHOR	112
ABOUT THE CONSULTANT	112

CHAPTER ONE

ITALY

In March 2020, the streets of most Italian towns and cities were quiet. No cars zipped down the roads, and no pedestrians walked to work, schools, or stores. The only sign of life on the streets was the occasional police officer or soldier who patrolled the area. The usual hustle and bustle of life in most Italian towns had come to a halt. All Italian citizens had been ordered to remain home unless they were essential workers, such as police or medical personnel.

Severe acute respiratory syndrome coronavirus 2 (SARS-CoV-2), the contagious virus that causes the disease COVID-19, was quickly spreading in Italy. Italian leaders scrambled to slow the infection rate and prevent the deaths of thousands of Italians. Between late February and March 9, more than 9,000 Italians had become infected. More than 460 people had died.[1] Most of those deaths were among elderly people. Italy's

During Italy's lockdown, places that were normally bustling with tourists and activity were deserted.

WHAT IS COVID-19?

COVID-19 is an infectious disease. It is caused by the SARS-CoV-2 virus. The virus causes mild to severe respiratory illness, and symptoms include coughing, sneezing, headache, fever, body chills, body aches, shortness of breath, and more. Many people experience loss of taste and smell. In severe cases, people have difficulty breathing. The virus spreads through particles when people cough, sneeze, talk, or breathe. COVID-19 affects people differently. Some people don't even know they're sick and never experience symptoms. But some become very sick and need to be hospitalized. COVID-19 can be deadly, especially to the elderly and those with weakened immune systems. However, even healthy young people may die from the disease.

leaders were nervous. The virus was deadlier to those who were elderly or sick. Italy was home to the continent's highest concentration of elderly people.

LOCKDOWN OF A COUNTRY

How could the country stop the spread of the deadly virus? Italy's prime minister, Giuseppe Conte, was willing to take drastic measures to reduce the infection rate.

On March 9, 2020, Conte announced in a news conference that Italy would enact measures to control the outbreak within its own borders. Schools, stores, museums, tourist sites, entertainment venues, and many other places would be closed. All public gatherings, including concerts, sporting events, weddings, and funerals, were banned.

Prime Minister Conte announced that for three weeks, people would be ordered to stay home and could travel only for work, health needs, or emergencies. Immediately, people flocked to supermarkets to panic buy groceries and other supplies.

The next day, the city of Milan, Italy's center of business and finance, looked deserted. In Rome, famous historical sites such as the Colosseum and the Pantheon were closed. Some confusion accompanied the lockdown. Italians wondered if they could leave their homes to walk their dogs. Schoolchildren remained home. Adults worked from home if they were able. The lockdown was a shock to everyday life for everyone.

By March 18, the number of COVID-19 cases in Italy jumped to 35,000. Nearly 3,000 Italians had died from the mysterious new virus.[2] And as the COVID-19 pandemic intensified around the world, many wondered how long it would last.

As cases of COVID-19 continued to climb, the lockdowns lasted into June. Throughout Italy, people did what they could to help each other through the isolation and loneliness of this time. A group of 200 psychologists formed a free mental health hotline to offer counseling

> "Interestingly, everyone in Italy is a cook again. In the absence of restaurants, it seems that more and more quarantined Italians are rediscovering age-old family recipes from their *nonne* (grandmothers) and sharing them across social media."[3]
>
> —Erica Firpo, journalist, Rome, Italy

over the phone to those battling isolation and depression. Chefs with closed restaurants volunteered to prepare meals for the homeless. Theater performers acted out livestreamed fairy tales to schoolchildren stuck at home. Young people volunteered to deliver groceries and medications to the elderly so they did not have to risk being exposed to COVID-19 by going to stores to pick up those supplies.

To boost morale, Italians turned to music. Each day, when the church bells in Rome chimed at 6:00 p.m., neighbors opened their windows and joined in singing classic Italian songs. Across the country, in towns and cities, neighborhood choruses sang the national anthem from their windows. Italians adopted a sense that they were all in it together, and people did their best to help their neighbors.

Italians looked for ways to keep their spirits up, such as singing together from their balconies.

THE HEALTH-CARE BATTLE

While the world had become quiet for many, it was a different story in Italy's overflowing hospitals. Francesco Longo, a researcher at Bocconi University's Centre for Research on Health and Social Care Management, said, "It seems relaxed because everyone is staying inside and people are cooking and looking at old photos and doing work at home. But in hospitals, it's like a war."[4] Like the rest of the world, Italy was not prepared for COVID-19. Hospitals did not have the medical equipment needed to help all the patients flooding in. COVID-19 is a respiratory illness that can attack the lungs. Many critical patients need ventilators. Ventilators are machines that assist patients with breathing when their lungs are too sick or damaged to do it themselves. But hospitals had only a small number of these machines. Doctors and nurses struggled with deciding which patients would receive a

Tentlike emergency structures provided additional space for overflowing Italian hospitals.

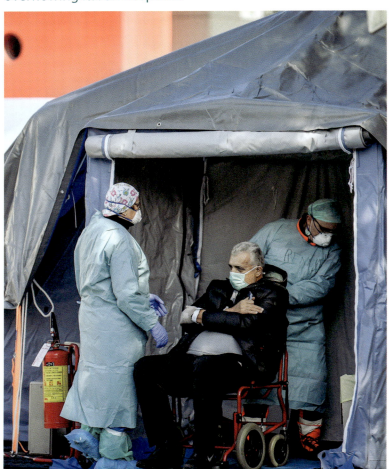

ventilator and which ones wouldn't. They also struggled with a shortage of personal protective equipment (PPE) such as hospital-grade masks, gowns, goggles, and face shields. PPE helps prevent the spread of disease between people. By mid-March 2020, hospitals were running out of beds, equipment, and people as health-care workers began to catch the virus. Some doctors and nurses died from the disease. Makeshift hospital units were set up to help COVID-19 patients. It seemed hopeless.

Crematoriums and cemeteries struggled to handle the growing number of bodies. Prime Minister Conte's decree meant funerals could not happen. Family members grieved at home as loved ones were buried alone, with no family gathered for a funeral. Priests gave a simple blessing before coffins were buried. The COVID-19 pandemic had become a nightmare in Italy.

THE START OF A PANDEMIC

SARS-CoV-2 was first detected in Wuhan in the province of Hubei, China, in late 2019. Several people became sick with a respiratory illness, but it was soon evident this was different than illnesses doctors normally treated. This one seemed deadlier. COVID-19 was first reported to the World Health Organization (WHO) on December 31, 2019. On January 30, 2020, the WHO declared COVID-19 a global health emergency. Although China had established lockdown procedures to keep the virus from spreading, COVID-19 had begun to travel around the world. Businesspeople and visitors traveling into and out of China unknowingly became infected and took the virus with them.

Within weeks, COVID-19 had spread to six continents. By December 2020, COVID-19 even reached Antarctica when 36 research scientists tested positive. Government leaders around the globe had to decide how to handle the spread. Some countries, such as Italy, went into lockdown. Others took a very relaxed approach, believing good handwashing and social distancing would

ANDRÀ TUTTO BENE

All schools and day care centers around Italy were closed during the lockdown. Some mothers in the town of Bari came up with a way to lift the spirits of neighborhood children stuck at home. Hand-painted rainbows began popping up in windows with the words *andrà tutto bene*, meaning "everything will be alright." The message of hope quickly spread throughout Italy. Painted rainbows appeared in shop windows, in neighborhoods, and on social media reminding people to not give up hope.

be enough. Social distancing is the practice of maintaining physical distance between individuals so the virus is less likely to spread from one person to the next. Within months, however, it was clear that COVID-19 wasn't going to go away on its own.

In December 2020, the first vaccines for COVID-19 were approved for emergency use in people 16 and older. But the pandemic was still not over. A handful of pharmaceutical companies created COVID-19 vaccines. Some vaccines required two doses. This meant that billions of doses of vaccine had to be manufactured and distributed. This would take time. By December 2021, many countries were still waiting to receive doses of vaccine to distribute.

COVID-19 GOES GLOBAL

Throughout most of 2020, Antarctica had managed to escape COVID-19's spread. But in December, Antarctica lost the privilege of being the only continent free of the virus when researchers at the Chilean Bernardo O'Higgins research station tested positive for COVID-19. Scientists and researchers began to worry about what that could mean for the wildlife in Antarctica should the virus make the jump from humans to animals there. Scientists continued to monitor the situation. On other continents, COVID-19 was later found in deer, hamsters, cats, and other animals.

A SLOW RETURN TO LIFE IN ITALY

In September 2020, Italian schools reopened to welcome children back to the classroom. Masks were mandatory unless students were eating or in gym class. Strict social distancing rules were enforced. The following spring, Italy reopened its borders to travelers.

The summer of 2021 saw the reopening of sports events, fairs, conferences, pools, and other public venues. A special pass was necessary to enter these places, as well as cafés and restaurants. To get a pass, people had to prove they had received at least one dose of a COVID-19 vaccine in the previous six months or had tested negative for COVID-19 in the last 48 hours.

By the end of 2021, more than 6.1 million Italians, or 10,147 of every 100,000 people, had been sick with COVID-19.[5] More than 137,000 of those infected died from complications due to the virus, bringing the number of deaths to 228 per 100,000 people in Italy.[6] But those numbers may have been greater had the country not gone into lockdown in March 2020. While the lockdown didn't completely stop the spread, it slowed it enough that hospitals were able to catch up. Many countries praised Italy for its quick response to the pandemic and for the attitude most Italians maintained throughout the quarantine. "I think that we'll remember the shock we felt in the first week of March for a very long time: the people taking to supermarkets in a panic, the hardships of the most vulnerable," said Stefano Marrone, a volunteer in Milan. "But we'll also remember the strength ordinary people had to react."[7]

1918 FLU PANDEMIC

The most severe pandemic in recent history was the influenza pandemic that spanned from 1918 to 1919. It was first identified in military personnel in 1918 but quickly spread to an estimated 500 million people, one-third of the world's population.[9] It was once called the Spanish flu because many falsely believed it had originated in Spain. Although its true origins are still unknown, scientists know that it was caused by an H1N1 virus that originated in birds and spread to humans. The 1918 flu had a high mortality rate among patients younger than five years old, those 20 to 40 years old, and those 65 and older. At the time, there was no vaccine to fight it and no antibiotics to treat the infections that influenza can cause. The only things people could do to try to survive the pandemic were to quarantine, use good hygiene such as handwashing, and avoid public gatherings.

The COVID-19 pandemic was the worst pandemic the world had experienced since the 1918 influenza pandemic. By 2022, more than 289 million people around the world had been infected with COVD-19.[8] More than 5.4 million of those people had died, which was approximately

COVID-19 BY THE NUMBERS

DEADLY PANDEMICS[10]

COVID-19 is not the first global pandemic to cause a large loss of life. Throughout history, pandemics have killed large numbers of people. In ancient times, people had very little medical knowledge to fight diseases. Although much was unknown about COVID-19 at the beginning of the outbreak, medical professionals were able to slow the spread and offer therapeutic assistance to those struggling with the disease. In comparison, during the spread of bubonic plague during the Black Death of the mid-1300s CE, little was known about hygiene, sanitation, and medicine in general. An estimated 40 percent of people in Europe died.[11] The graphic shows how COVID-19 stacks up against other major pandemics that have occurred throughout history.

Yersinia pestis

Influenza virus

Human immunodeficiency virus

SARS-CoV-2

PATHOGEN	ILLNESS	YEARS	DEATHS
Yersinia pestis	Bubonic plague	1347–1351	75–200 million
Influenza virus	Influenza	1918–1919	40–50 million
Human immunodeficiency virus	HIV/AIDS	1981–present	24–35 million
SARS-CoV-2	COVID-19	2019–present	6.2 million (through early April 2022)

69 deaths for every 100,000 people.[12] While scientists and health-care workers made great strides, the pandemic was still not over heading into 2022. In fact, the virus had mutated into a handful of different variants. When a virus changes slightly, or mutates, it's considered a new variant. Changes can include how quickly it spreads, how serious disease symptoms are, how well a vaccine works against it, and other things. World leaders and governments around the globe took their own approaches to fighting the disease. Government leaders had to decide which steps would work best for their own countries and implement plans to keep their citizens safe while not destroying the economy. It was not an easy task, but some leaders were noticing what was working and what was not working in other countries and then applying the effective strategies at home.

CHAPTER TWO

CHINA

The first case of what would become known as COVID-19 was reported in December 2019 in Wuhan, a city of 11 million people.[1] Doctors did not know at the time that they were dealing with a new virus. The patient had pneumonia-like symptoms, including fever, cough, and difficulty breathing, but that did not raise an alarm. Within a week, however, more people began seeking medical treatment for similar symptoms. Later, researchers looked back on the first cases and determined that they were COVID-19 illnesses.

The virus spread quickly. From December 1 to December 29, more than 180 patients sought medical treatment for the same illness, but doctors weren't exactly sure what it was.[2] A number of the cases seemed linked to a seafood market in Wuhan. On December 31, China reported the possibility of a new virus to the WHO. The report stated that doctors weren't certain

Wuhan is located in eastern China.

how the disease was transmitted. Some doctors thought the illness was not transmitted from human to human, only from animal to human. All of the patients were placed in quarantine while medical personnel worked to find answers.

On January 1, 2020, the Chinese Center for Disease Control and Prevention closed the Huanan Seafood

Huanan Seafood Wholesale Market was closed so authorities could investigate the new illness.

Wholesale Market in Wuhan. Police oversaw workers closing their booths. Health officials collected samples from surfaces throughout the market. They also tried to raise awareness among livestock farmers of the importance of sanitation. Two days later, Chinese authorities told labs and hospitals to destroy all laboratory samples from patients with this new virus, saying this would help prevent infections.

News went out on Chinese social media alerting people that an outbreak of an unknown disease was happening in Wuhan. China's public security bureau arrested eight people for spreading what it called rumors. Panic mounted as people feared that a deadly respiratory disease called severe acute respiratory syndrome (SARS) had made a comeback. SARS is a serious disease. An outbreak occurred in China in 2003 that spread to other areas of the world.

China made the official announcement on January 7, 2020, that scientists had identified the virus as a novel, or new, coronavirus, a family of viruses that also cause the common cold and flu. Scientists initially named the new virus 2019-nCoV. While it was very similar to the SARS virus, there were differences. The samples

DR. LI WENLIANG, WHISTLEBLOWER

At the start of the COVID-19 spread, the Chinese government censored information that was shared on social media. People were confused about what was happening, and rumors started to spread. Doctors were reprimanded and ordered to remain silent about what they were seeing in clinics and hospitals. They could not even warn each other or share information to try to treat the infected. Dr. Li Wenliang was one of these doctors. Li was an ophthalmologist working at a hospital in Wuhan. He heard of patients at his hospital with what might be SARS. He used an online chat group to send a warning to other doctors on December 30, 2019, advising them to use protective gear to avoid becoming infected. Four days later, he was brought before China's public security bureau and accused of making false comments that had "severely disturbed public order."[3] Li died the following month from COVID-19. After his death, Chinese officials apologized to his family for how they had handled the situation.

health officials had collected from the Wuhan market came back positive for this new virus. Neighboring countries began to take precautions. Japan started to screen travelers from Wuhan. Those with fevers or flu-like symptoms were placed in quarantine.

Midway through January, COVID-19 was identified outside of China when a case popped up in Thailand on January 13. The following day, Chinese health officials admitted in a private meeting that human-to-human spread was possible, and they began emergency preparations for a pandemic. But they understated how severe or transmissible the virus was to the public. Instead of warning the people of Wuhan to stay home, they said people could still celebrate the upcoming Lunar New Year. Millions of people travel to and from Wuhan every year for the celebrations. Lunar New Year festivities went ahead as normal through January 22. Throngs of people gathered for festivals and parades.

Large crowds of people came to Wuhan for the 2020 Lunar New Year celebrations.

Many would unknowingly be taking the virus with them and spreading it to family and friends in other parts of China.

LOCKDOWNS BEGIN

On January 23, Wuhan began a strict lockdown. The central government of China sent out notices to people's smartphones at 2:00 a.m. letting them know airport, train, and bus travel would be shut down at 10:00 a.m. People rushed to supermarkets and pharmacies. They stocked up on basic necessities such as rice, noodles, and eggs. Rubbing alcohol and disinfectants were sold out on pharmacy shelves. The streets of Wuhan became empty and quiet. The city's 11 million people were quarantined at home. One person from each family was allowed to leave home once

"NOT ENOUGH"

The suddenness of the lockdown in Wuhan caused anxiety for many people. Wang Ying, who went out in the large crowds on New Year's Eve that the Chinese government had allowed, said, "I am a bit panicked because before the government said it wasn't serious so no one thought it was a big deal. Then this morning, Wuhan was suddenly sealed off. I think the government's early warnings were not enough."[4]

every three days for groceries and supplies. Face masks and social distancing were required for those leaving their homes.

A 29-year-old social worker named Guo Jing kept a diary of her lockdown experience. In it, she wrote on January 23, "I went to a pharmacy and it was already limiting the number of shoppers. It had already sold out of masks and alcohol disinfectant. After stocking up on food, I am still in shock. Cars and pedestrians are dwindling, and the city has come to a stop all out of a sudden. When will the city live again?"[5]

Within a week, thousands of people in Wuhan were sick and flooding the hospitals. Makeshift field hospitals were built to help house patients sick with the

> **TAKING WHAT THEY CAN GET**
>
> Some Wuhan residents found it very difficult to get groceries during the lockdown. Neighbors discovered they had a better chance of getting certain foods from grocery stores if they combined their needs and ordered larger amounts through group messaging apps. Certain districts began to regulate group delivery services, forcing supermarkets to sell in bulk to neighborhoods instead of to individual customers. Wuhan resident Guo Jing reported that group ordering was the only way she was able to get food, but she could not choose which fruits and vegetables she wanted to buy. "You cannot have personal preferences anymore," she said.[6]

new virus. Eventually, conference centers and gymnasiums were converted into emergency medical treatment centers. Days after the Wuhan lockdown was announced, the entire province of Hubei was put into lockdown too.

Authorities in Wuhan strictly enforced stay-at-home orders. They went door-to-door to perform health checks. Anyone showing symptoms was removed from the home and taken to quarantine facilities. Government officials required apartment building caretakers to monitor the temperatures of all residents. Outside, drones hovered overhead, scolding anyone not wearing a face mask and telling people to get back indoors. Throughout the city, facial-recognition software was used and linked to a mandatory phone app. The software allowed people into stores and public spaces based on their risk of exposure.

> "We couldn't go outside under any circumstances. Not even if you have a pet. Those with dogs had to play with them inside and teach them to use the bathroom in a certain spot."[7]
>
> —Wang Jingjun, 27-year-old graduate student

The lockdown successfully slowed the spread of COVID-19 in Wuhan. On April 8, 2020, the lockdown was lifted. The people of Wuhan had spent 76 days in lockdown.[8] The city put on a sound-and-light show to applaud the efforts of the people and to celebrate the courage and sacrifice of first responders. Three months after COVID-19 began to spread through Wuhan, the local transmission appeared to be under control. But it was too late to completely stop the spread. By March 8, more than 100 countries around the world were reporting cases of COVID-19. A few days later, COVID-19 had been labeled a global pandemic.

HONG KONG

Hong Kong, a city of nearly 7.5 million, was the most visited city in the world in 2019. Hong Kong is connected to mainland China but is considered a special administrative region of the People's Republic of China. It has been allowed to manage its own affairs since it was granted its independence from British colonial rule in 1997. Hong Kong's economy is heavily dependent on tourism. But with the arrival of COVID-19 and lockdowns in China, Hong Kong saw its tourism decline more than 97 percent in 2021. With more than 260,000 people in Hong Kong employed by the tourism and service industries, closed borders and lockdowns took a huge toll on the city.[9]

CHAPTER THREE

ASIA

The island nation Taiwan spent 2020 with one of the world's lowest rates per capita of COVID-19. As the pandemic began spreading through Asia, Taiwan went about business as usual. Schools remained open, concerts played, and theaters were packed. As a group of small islands, it was easier for Taiwan's government to control people entering or exiting the country than for places with shared borders, and therefore it was easier to limit the potential number of COVID-positive people coming to the island.

The country established tight border control and enforced strict quarantine rules for anyone who contracted the disease. Taiwan barred foreigners from entering the islands, with a few exceptions for those finishing up business contracts. Those admitted had to spend 14 days in quarantine upon arrival. The first confirmed case of COVID-19 in Taiwan was on

Taiwanese people continued to enjoy food from the night markets through 2020. However, the markets received less business than in a usual year because of the pandemic.

January 21, 2020. The patient was a 50-year-old woman who had been teaching in Wuhan. In April, Taiwan instituted mask mandates for public transportation. Later, it extended the mask mandate to everyone on the island. All citizens were required to wear masks outside their homes.

As cases began to climb in October 2020, the government of Taiwan required anyone entering the country to show proof of a negative COVID-19 test. Thorough contact tracing was performed for positive cases of COVID-19. Contact tracing is a process that involves public health workers figuring out all the people exposed to an infected person and then contacting those people so they can quarantine, monitor themselves for symptoms, and know what to do if they start experiencing symptoms. This slowed the spread of infection. The country's efforts paid off. Throughout 2020, Taiwan experienced a much smaller number of COVID-19 cases than other industrialized countries around the world. On October 29, Taiwan reached the milestone of 200 days without local transmission of the virus. The country ended 2020 with only seven COVID-19 deaths.[1]

One of Taiwan's early successes was its ability to quickly produce masks and other supplies needed for the pandemic.

Heading into the winter of 2020–2021, with cases around the world on the rise, Taiwan enforced new protocols. Masks were to be worn in all high-risk areas. Anyone caught not adhering to the mask requirements was fined. In addition, the government asked for all medical institutions and local governments to assist with screening patients.

In January 2021, when a cluster of new cases turned up at Taoyuan General Hospital, Taiwan's army deployed troops from its 33rd Chemical Warfare Group. Armed with backpack sprayers, the soldiers sprayed disinfectant and bleach in areas with confirmed cases. Taiwanese citizens

> **LUNAR NEW YEAR FESTIVALS CANCELED**
>
> In 2021, Taiwan canceled its Lantern Festival, an event that marks the end of Lunar New Year celebrations, as government officials were concerned a spike in COVID-19 cases would arise. The government's top priority was to keep cases to a minimum, even if that meant forgoing beloved celebrations. Although the people of Taiwan weren't able to gather for the yearly festival, artwork from the festival was still displayed for people to enjoy.

greeted the soldiers with cheers and messages such as "Keep up the good work, soldier brothers" and "Thank you for defending our home."[2]

On March 22, 2021, the first doses of COVID-19 vaccines were administered. All Taiwanese people could get vaccinated for free. Health-care workers were the first to receive vaccines. By the end of December 2021, 68 percent of Taiwan had been fully vaccinated against COVID-19.[3]

INDIA

While Taiwan was able to get ahead of things and control the spread of COVID-19, India wasn't as fortunate. The first wave of COVID-19 hit India on January 30, 2020, when three Indian medical students tested positive after returning from Wuhan. India's first wave was relatively mild compared with other areas of the world. The government imposed a nationwide lockdown on March 25, 2020, which lasted through May. This helped slow the spread of the disease. But it also led to an economic crisis. Millions of people lost their jobs. A majority of jobs in India, as in other countries with emerging and developing economies, are in the informal sector. Informal sector jobs are typically unregistered and not protected by the government. They include occupations that take relatively little training, such as clearing trash from streets or selling goods as a street vendor. Many of these people were

VACCINES AND BOOSTERS

Most vaccines work by prompting the body to form an antibody response to the target antigen, such as a virus or bacteria. The body will remember that antigen in the future. If a vaccinated person becomes infected, the body's immune system is ready to attack. At the beginning of 2022, guidelines from the US Centers for Disease Control and Prevention and the WHO called for fully vaccinated people to receive a booster shot five months after their last vaccination. It was discovered that the one- and two-dose COVID-19 vaccines became less effective over time. Booster shots helped restore protection against severe illness from COVID-19. Doctors and researchers in Israel spearheaded research into the effectiveness of a fourth vaccine booster shot. They concluded that the fourth shot does increase antibodies more than just the third, but not enough to prevent infection from the Omicron variant, which was the dominant variant heading into 2022. The fourth shot was still very effective against the Alpha and Delta variants, however.

COVID-19 hit low-wage workers in India the hardest, leading to either less income or increased risk of illness.

unable to work because of the pandemic, and without work, they didn't get paid. Oftentimes, people with manual labor jobs do not make much money. They live paycheck to paycheck with little money in savings. Simply being able to afford food and rent became very difficult. Many of these people remained out of work even as the first wave passed.

The second wave of COVID-19 hit India much harder. It began in March 2021. Many people in India live in large, densely populated cities. This makes social distancing and isolating difficult. Additionally, India's health-care system isn't adequate for the number of people living there. When cases began to ramp up, those infected had a difficult time getting into overrun hospitals for care. Many hospitals ran out of oxygen canisters for patients having difficulty breathing because of COVID-19.

India's prime minister Narendra Modi deployed military aircraft and activated trains to deliver oxygen tanks and supplies to areas struggling with shortages. But it wasn't enough. Many areas never received any of these much-needed supplies. Cases soared. Many Indians felt abandoned by their government.

Clinics, hospitals, and care facilities struggled to keep up with the patient load. By late April 2021, daily infection rates hit 300,000 new cases a day. Nearly 18 million people in India had become infected with COVID-19. Russia, the

NO OXYGEN

In April and May 2021, many COVID-19 patients in India died because of an insufficient supply of supplemental oxygen. The number of cases and the lack of medical infrastructure had taken a toll on just about everything needed to combat the pandemic, including hospital beds, test kits, and medicine. Hospitals had run out of oxygen canisters to fill with oxygen. Families of COVID-19 patients became so desperate to get their loved ones on oxygen that they began searching for empty canisters they could fill. When it was revealed that there was no data about how many had died because of a lack of oxygen, people took to social media, outraged and asking for help.

DEALING WITH THE DEAD

The large number of COVID-19 deaths in India throughout the second wave in 2021 caused new issues with burials and cremations. The need became so great that crematoriums had a very difficult time keeping up with the demand. Several crematoriums and graveyards in the city of Surat had three times more cremations and burials than usual. Delhi made makeshift crematoriums for the sheer number of deaths in the city, even going so far as to use parking lots to make more room. Workers were burning remains around the clock, causing problems with smoke and heat. In some instances, they had to burn 30 to 40 bodies at a time.[6]

United Kingdom, New Zealand, France, and the United States all pledged to send emergency medical supplies. May 1 set a record of more than 400,000 new COVID-19 cases reported in a single day.[4] Anurag Agrawal, a doctor and medical researcher in New Delhi, India, explained that large public gatherings and celebrations had been a key factor in the spread. Since February of that year, people had grown more comfortable, thinking the worst was behind them. They were eager to get on with their lives and end lockdowns. "Functions, marriages that had been delayed for a year were suddenly held day, after day, after day," Agrawal explained.[5]

Between the end of April and late May 2021, India jumped from a total of 200,000 deaths related to COVID-19 since the beginning of the pandemic to 300,000, or 21.8 deaths per 100,000 people.[7] Crematoriums struggled to keep up with disposal of the bodies. Family members resorted to burning them in the streets. Experts believe that India's official COVID-19 death toll is likely significantly undercounted.

Vaccines were first available to frontline workers in January 2021. In April, shortly after people age 18 and older were allowed to get vaccinated, a government website where Indians could register crashed soon after launching. It was another blow to a country that was already dealing with a catastrophic situation. By the end of 2021, just over 43 percent of India's population was fully vaccinated.[8] The percentage continued to climb into 2022, prompting health officials to hope that India would experience fewer COVID-related deaths moving forward.

> "These days I don't even get two hours of sleep. At 7 a.m. I come here, I start dispatching ambulances, or I arrange for a dead body to be picked up, then get it cremated."[9]
>
> —Jitender Singh Shunty, New Delhi crematorium worker

CHAPTER FOUR

AUSTRALIA AND NEW ZEALAND

On January 25, 2020, the first case of COVID-19 in Australia was recorded in the country's second-largest city, Melbourne. Over the next several weeks, a growing number of Australian tourists returning from China tested positive. By March, the number of travelers and tourists entering Australia who tested positive for COVID-19 grew a concerning amount.

In early March, the Australian government restricted travelers from China, Iran, South Korea, and Italy. By March 20, the government banned all travelers coming into Australia who were not Australian residents returning home from abroad. This put a stop to international tourism in Australia. On March 28, a mandatory two-week hotel quarantine policy was enacted for anyone flying into Australia. Australia's eight

Scott Morrison became prime minister of Australia in August 2018.

states also closed their borders to travel between states to help prevent the spread of COVID-19.

Daily case numbers continued to climb. Australia's prime minister Scott Morrison gathered state leaders to discuss an action plan to help stop the spread of the virus. Schools switched to online learning. Non-essential businesses closed. Restaurants, cafés, and stores stayed open for to-go orders. Any Australians who were able to stay home or work from home did so. The partial lockdown seemed to be working as cases fell from approximately 400 new cases a day in March to fewer than 20 cases a day in May.[1]

> "Essential workers are being forced to put themselves in harm's way to keep food on the shelves, medicines in stock, the lights and water on and keep this country open for business."[2]
> —Sally McManus, secretary of the Australian Council of Trade Unions

STRICT LOCKDOWNS

Australia's borders remained closed to international travelers in June 2020, but its internal lockdowns were eased for Australians, leading to a rise in cases. Most of the new cases were around Melbourne, in the state of Victoria. Areas of Melbourne with high numbers of positive cases were put into lockdown. Within a month, the government enacted a strict lockdown for all of Melbourne as cases began to surge to more than 100 new cases a day. Stores, childcare facilities, and businesses closed. Strict rules were enforced. Face masks were required indoors and outdoors. One person per family was allowed to shop. Outdoor exercise was limited to one hour each day. No one was allowed to be outdoors after 8:00 p.m., and travel was restricted to a three-mile (5 km) radius.[3] In July, state borders stayed open except to Victoria. The hope was that the spread of the virus could be contained.

TROUBLE AT THE BORDERS

In July 2020, Australian states imposed strict border restrictions. Because cases of COVID-19 were rising fast in the state of Victoria, neighboring states banned travel to and from Victoria. This caused a number of hardships for those living close to the border. Some people normally commuted across state lines for work. Suddenly, these people, even some health-care workers, were not able to get to their jobs. People in rural areas sometimes relied on towns or cities across the border for groceries and other necessities. Some people were left without access to their clinics and doctors. The last time state border closures had happened was in 1919, when the 1918 influenza pandemic arrived in the country.

Between July and October 2020, cases in Australia surged. Strict lockdowns were kept in place. New cases of COVID-19 had decreased enough by November that the lockdown ended and shops and restaurants reopened.

FORTRESS AUSTRALIA AND QUARANTINE CAMPS

In February 2021, COVID-19 vaccines became available in Australia. Many Australians were willing to get vaccinated, but the rollout was slow. Health-care workers and the elderly were the first to be vaccinated. Australia didn't aim for a swift mass vaccination of everyone, but rather a slower paced, gradual vaccination. The country had very few cases of COVID-19 during the first half of 2021, and life returned to normal for many Australians.

While cases of COVID-19 exploded around the world, Australia was seeing very

MAIL GOES UNDELIVERED

With many shops closed because of lockdowns, Australians began ordering far more supplies online, causing the Australian mail to become hugely overburdened. Capacities were so greatly strained that for a while, Australia stopped accepting packages coming in from other countries. Frustrated family and loved ones told stories of sending care packages to Australia, only to have them returned undelivered.

few new cases. This led people to call their island country Fortress Australia. But in June, one case of the new Delta variant of COVID-19 was discovered in Sydney. With only 5 percent of Australians vaccinated at the time, the Delta variant began spreading rapidly. More than half of Australia's population of 25 million found themselves back in lockdown. Professor Michael Toole from the medical research center Burnet Institute explained: "We were in a bit of a COVID-free paradise. And I think it led to a level of complacency, both within the government and among the public. . . . Now, it's all a mess."[4]

Quarantine camps were built to isolate travelers and those who had been infected or exposed to the virus. These sites, called centers for national resilience, housed about 2,000 people in small dormitory rooms. Stays were 14 days long, and individuals were charged for their two-week stay, which included food. Many people at the quarantine camps near Howard Springs, Brisbane, and Melbourne believed the camps would help lessen the spread of COVID-19. Others felt forced into a prison-type situation, with some trying to escape the facilities.

Economists figured lockdowns throughout the summer cost the Australian economy more than

Australia sometimes used hotels as quarantine locations for people flying into the country.

$17 billion in Australian currency ($12.5 billion in US dollars).[5] As more people were faced with the seriousness of the disease and lockdowns, vaccination rates began rising. By the end of October 2021, things had improved. Officials had promised residents of Victoria that the lockdown would be lifted once 70 percent of the state was fully vaccinated. On October 22, the government lifted the lockdown. It had been the world's longest lockdown, with the people of Victoria isolated in their homes under stay-at-home orders for a total of 262 days in two long stretches from July to October 2020 and August to October 2021.[6] Vaccination rates in other states, such as Western Australia, were not as high as Victoria because there were few cases of COVID-19. This led some to believe they didn't need to be vaccinated. By November 1, 2021, the states of Victoria and New South Wales had hit high enough vaccination rates that they both opened to international travelers.

On December 31, 2021, the Australian Department of Health reported a total of 395,504 cases of COVID-19 in Australia since the beginning of the pandemic, with a total of 2,239 deaths.[7] Although Australia had faced two large surges by the end of 2021, it was well behind other countries in terms of numbers of positive cases. Australia averaged nine deaths per 100,000 people.[8]

NEW ZEALAND

Across the Tasman Sea to the southeast of Australia, New Zealand recorded its first COVID-19 case on February 28, 2020. An infected person had arrived in New Zealand from Iran. The news that a COVID-19–positive case had been identified reached the people of New Zealand the next day. New Zealanders flocked to stores to stock up on canned food, toilet paper, and other essentials. The New Zealand government restricted all travelers from Iran.

Within two weeks, six confirmed cases of COVID-19 had been identified. The government announced travelers arriving in New Zealand would have to self-isolate for 14 days. Cruise ships were banned from docking in New Zealand. But for the rest of the island country, life continued as normal. No lockdowns or stay-at-home orders were enacted. People continued to go to work and school and gather for social events.

The *Golden Princess* cruise ship had arrived in New Zealand before the cruise ship ban, but its passengers were still not allowed to disembark because of suspected COVID-19 cases onboard.

A TURN FOR THE WORSE

By March 19, a total of 28 cases of COVID-19 were confirmed in New Zealand. Each of those cases was linked to overseas travel. The government believed this meant that the virus was not yet spreading within the community. It announced a ban on all indoor gatherings of more than 100 people.[9] Additionally, it closed the country's borders for the first time in history. The only people allowed into New Zealand were citizens and permanent residents returning from overseas.

The New Zealand government put together a relief package. It was worth $12.1 billion in New Zealand dollars ($7.3 billion in US dollars), including $500 million for health care, $8.7 billion to support jobs and businesses, and $2.8 billion to replace lost income and to boost consumer spending.[10] As more cases popped up in Auckland, New Zealand's capital and largest city, the city closed pools, libraries, and museums. The following day, more cases made it clear that the virus was spreading throughout the community.

New Zealand prime minister Jacinda Ardern requested that New Zealanders 70 years of age and older and those with compromised immune systems stay home. She also encouraged people to work from home if they were able. A four-level alert system was introduced to help people know the current risk of community transmission. On March 24, 2020, the country reached level 3, and schools and all non-essential businesses closed. Pharmacies, clinics, and grocery stores remained open. Two days later, the country moved to level 4, and it went into four weeks of lockdown. "In the face of the greatest threat to human health that we have faced in over a century, [New Zealanders] have quietly and collectively implemented a nationwide wall of defence," Ardern said on April 9, a couple of weeks into the lockdown. "You are breaking the chain of transmission and you did it for each other."[11]

The country went from May 22 to June 15 without reporting a single new case. Following that, nearly all positive cases recorded were people returning home after international travel. They were put in mandatory isolation centers, which stopped potential spread. In September, the government restricted gatherings in Auckland to just ten people, causing a large anti-lockdown protest. The number of active cases was at 77, or an average of 1.5 people per 100,000. By comparison, the number of

Jacinda Ardern, *center left*, stands with electorate workers without masks or social distancing. At various points in 2020, New Zealand did not require these measures because of low spread of the virus.

global cases was nearly 30 million, an average of nearly four people per 100,000.[12] In October, the New Zealand government arranged to purchase vaccine doses of the Pfizer-BioNTech COVID-19 vaccine. The remainder of 2020 brought more positive cases. In December, the New Zealand government announced even more funding would be dedicated to testing, contact tracing, and isolation.

In February 2021, the Ministry of Social Development began paying workers waiting for COVID-19 test results who were unable to work from home. That same month, the Pfizer-BioNTech vaccine began to be administered to nurses, security personnel, and cleaners at a hotel being used for quarantined people in Auckland. Health-care and border workers were next up to receive the vaccine, and the general public became eligible for the shot later that year. Throughout 2021, the country moved between levels 1, 2, and 3 of lockdown, depending on the number of active cases. The vaccine rolled out, although more slowly than hoped.

Until August 2021, the New Zealand government had hoped to eliminate COVID-19 in the country. But when the more contagious Delta variant began to spread that month, it became clear the island nation would have to learn to live with the virus. The government established the COVID-19 Protection Framework, also known as the Traffic Light System, which rated regions as red, orange, or green, depending on their level of exposure to the virus and vaccination rates. Level red required mandatory face masks in public places and limits on the number of people who could gather. Level orange saw a return to a lot of regular activities, such as events and gatherings, but face masks were required in shopping outlets and on public transportation. Level green had nearly no restrictions.

At the beginning of 2022, 75 percent of New Zealanders were fully vaccinated.[13] The country's tight border restrictions and geographic location helped limit the spread of COVID-19. The country had reported about 14,000 positive cases of COVID-19 and 51 deaths, resulting in an average of one death per 100,000 people.[14]

VACCINE ROLLOUT FOR MĀORI PEOPLE

Although New Zealand's vaccine rollout was successful, some criticized it for being inequitable. The Māori people are Indigenous people of New Zealand. Vaccination rates for elderly Māori hit 92 percent in October 2021, just under the 94 percent rate for elderly people who were not Māori. But for those younger than 35, only 48 percent of Māori were at least partially vaccinated, compared with nearly 80 percent of white New Zealanders.[15] This was problematic because the Māori population is very young. With a low vaccination rate, COVID-19 could still spread easily and quickly through the population. The Waitangi Tribunal, which makes rulings based on claims brought by the Māori people against the government, stated the vaccine rollout had failed the Māori people by not adjusting the vaccination age requirements to get an adequate percentage of the population vaccinated.

CHAPTER FIVE

EUROPE

In Europe, Italy experienced an early and rapid increase of COVID-19 cases at the beginning of the pandemic. Germany took warning and had a plan in place before the disease was discovered there. The first positive case of COVID-19 was found on January 27, 2020, in the state of Bavaria near the city of Munich. Within six weeks, COVID-19 had spread to all of Germany's 16 states. On March 8, 2020, the first COVID-related death was registered in Germany.

On March 18, German chancellor Angela Merkel made a televised announcement. She warned the German people, "It is serious. So, please take it seriously. Since German reunification—no, since World War II [1939–1945]—our country has never faced a challenge that has so urgently required us to pull together in solidarity with each other."[1] A few days later, Germany

The Charité hospital in Berlin, Germany, was important to helping the country through the pandemic.

PASS THE SALT

Careful investigation in Germany allowed the government to pinpoint the exact moment COVID-19 was passed from human to human in Germany. A Chinese employee on a business trip to a Bavarian car parts company headquarters asked another employee to pass the saltshaker at the lunch table. Later, forensic research showed this employee may have been the one who had introduced COVID-19 to the workplace. The employee who passed the saltshaker contracted the virus.

followed Italy's example and locked down the country in one of the strictest lockdowns in all of Europe. Only essential businesses stayed open. By mid-April, wearing face masks in public became mandatory throughout Germany.

PREPARING FOR THE WORST

Germany's health-care system proved to be more prepared for disaster than those in other European countries. It had enough beds and ventilators for people struggling with severe COVID-19 symptoms, and unlike in Italy, the hospitals were not overwhelmed. In January 2020, Berlin's Charité hospital developed one of the first tests capable of diagnosing COVID-19. Public and private laboratories worked together to rapidly increase testing capabilities, which allowed people to know if they had COVID-19 so they could take steps to avoid infecting others. Scientists from Germany's University of Bonn developed and conducted early COVID-19 antibody studies. These tests can detect if a person has had COVID-19 at some point and if that person has immunity against becoming infected again.

Within weeks, Chancellor Merkel was getting pressure from state politicians to reopen the country. The number of cases was going down. The aggressive lockdown and social distancing had seemed to work. Millions of Germans had downloaded a smartphone app called Corona-Warn-App that allowed the public health department to conduct contact tracing. Cautiously, Merkel agreed to lift some restrictions. Schools and restaurants reopened in May 2020.

But by June, the number of positive COVID-19 cases in Germany had risen to more than 190,000. Nearly 9,000 deaths were attributed to COVID-19.[2] Authorities discovered clusters of infections in meatpacking plants and apartment buildings. German health officials sprang into action, setting up COVID-19 testing sites and quarantining individuals who had been exposed.

As the fall of 2020 approached, cases continued to rise, with the total number of deaths in Germany at 10,000 by October 24.[3] Just before Christmas, lockdowns were

> "Come alone, don't linger too long, keep your distance and shop at quiet times."[5]
> —Authorities in the Netherlands in December 2020, cautioning people about Christmas shopping in crowded city centers

reinstated. Merkel cited Christmas shopping as one of the reasons for a rise in COVID-19 cases. With many businesses being forced to close again, German finance minister Olaf Scholz announced businesses would receive monthly payments from the government.

At the beginning of 2021, vaccinations became available in Germany. Medical workers and the elderly were the first people eligible to receive the shot. By that summer, all adults in Germany were able to get vaccinated. In November, unvaccinated people who had to quarantine because of COVID-19 lost the right to receive sick pay. By the end of 2021, cases were once again climbing as the Omicron variant hit Germany. The vaccines were not as effective against preventing infection with the Omicron variant, but they did help prevent severe illness. Just under 71 percent of the German population was fully vaccinated.[4] With rising cases, Germany's newly elected chancellor Olaf Scholz warned on January 7, 2022, "Anyone who has an opportunity to get vaccinated shouldn't just go there, but rather run there."[6]

UNITED KINGDOM

The United Kingdom learned some difficult lessons as the pandemic hit. The first positive cases of COVID-19 were discovered on January 31, 2020. Early on, British scientists suggested herd immunity could be a beneficial approach. Herd immunity is achieved when enough people within a population get vaccinated or become sick and recover and develop antibodies. Because antibodies prevent people from getting sick again, the virus stops spreading in the population.

Weeks after COVID-19 began to spread in the United Kingdom, it became evident that simply waiting for herd

GERMANY CANCELS OKTOBERFEST

Every year, the city of Munich in Bavaria celebrates Oktoberfest. It is a folk festival with traditional German beverages, food, music, dancing, games, and revelry. It takes place over about 16 days from late September to early October. Around six million visitors from around the world come to Munich every year to enjoy Germany's famous Oktoberfest. But because of the rising number of cases of COVID-19 and the inability to socially distance at a crowded festival, Oktoberfest 2020 was canceled for the first time since World War II. The following year, Oktoberfest 2021 was canceled as well. Bavaria's minister-president Markus Söder explained: "It hurts, it's such a pity. We have agreed that the risk is simply too high."[7]

immunity wouldn't work. On March 23, 2020, the United Kingdom's prime minister Boris Johnson announced a stay-at-home order. All non-essential travel was banned. Schools closed, as did businesses, entertainment venues, and other gathering places. The British people were told to socially distance and to stay home and isolate if they didn't feel well. The medical community hurried to prepare hospitals and temporary critical care units, despite a shortage of PPE. Testing sites were set up, but the country scrambled with testing supply shortages. More than 1,000 people in the country had already died from COVID-19, with an average of more than 2,000 people testing positive every day.[8]

By the end of April, Prime Minister Johnson announced that the country was experiencing fewer hospital admissions and he believed they had flattened the curve and passed the peak of the pandemic crisis. *Flattening the curve* is a term meaning to slow the spread of a disease. Instead of many people getting sick at once in a short period of time, the number of infections is spread over a greater period of time. As a result, the number of people requiring health care at one time doesn't bombard the health-care system. Social distancing, handwashing, and using face masks all help with flattening the curve. But COVID-19 had claimed the lives of more than 36,000 people in the United Kingdom, and cases continued to climb.[9]

In May of 2020, the country introduced a program called Test and Trace. It was funded by the government and run by the UK Health Security Agency. The purpose of Test and Trace was to provide testing sites and to alert people if they had tested positive or to let people know if they had come in contact with infected people.

The Test and Trace service launched in September 2020.

Individuals who tested positive were instructed to isolate. Contact tracers identified those who had been exposed. Those people were then contacted and told to self-isolate for ten days.

The Test and Trace system got off to a slow and chaotic start. By November, UK leaders had no choice but to enforce a national lockdown. Cases were surging. The following month, rollout of COVID-19 vaccines began in the United Kingdom. Those in the highest risk categories—the elderly and those with compromised immune systems—were the first to receive the shots. By January 2022, 70 percent of UK residents had been fully vaccinated.[10] The United Kingdom had reported 148,891 deaths due to COVID-19, or approximately 218 deaths per 100,000 people.[11]

SWEDEN

Sweden took a similar approach to the United Kingdom's early response in handling the pandemic. Instead of lockdowns, the leaders in Sweden thought it would be best to remain open and allow citizens to decide for themselves whether they should isolate or use masks. Government health officials believed the elderly and those with medical conditions that put them at risk would choose to stay home. Meanwhile, younger and healthier Swedes might contract COVID-19, but leaders believed that these people would experience only mild systems. They thought allowing the young and healthy to get COVID-19 would ultimately create herd immunity, which would be important because there was no vaccine against COVID-19 at the time and therefore no way to prevent people from getting sick without isolating. By keeping the country open instead of forcing businesses to close,

Entering the pandemic, Sweden left it up to individuals to determine what preventative measures they wanted to take.

government leaders also felt they could avoid harming the economy.

Many scientists in Sweden supported the idea of attempting herd immunity as opposed to locking down the entire country and putting the economy at risk. But some disease experts warned this approach could result in unnecessary deaths. Sweden's government decided that herd immunity was worth a try. Sweden had the most relaxed COVID-19 rules in all of Europe. It didn't enforce a lockdown, schools and businesses did not close, and the government didn't create travel bans. But just weeks into the pandemic, thousands of Swedes were dead because of COVID-19. The country was forced to institute some lockdowns, such as the closure of high schools from March to June 2020, and again in December of that year, to prevent more deaths before vaccines were ready to roll out. But those were minor compared with what other countries were doing. Sweden never made masks mandatory. Anders Tegnell, the chief architect of Sweden's coronavirus strategy, was reluctant to take away personal freedoms. "You can't open and close schools," he said. "That is going to be a disaster." He said nationwide lockdowns would be like "using a hammer to kill a fly."[12]

But a year into the pandemic, some professionals in the medical and science fields criticized their government's approach to COVID-19. "They underestimated the mortality tremendously," said Claudia Hanson, an associate professor at Sweden's Karolinska Institutet. "Sweden became a dream for many people to think one can do it differently," Hanson explained. But looking back, she said, "It was maybe not a good idea."[13] Others have praised Sweden's approach, saying it was business-friendly and prevented economic destruction.

By August 2021, Sweden had recorded more cases of COVID-19 per capita than most other countries. Approximately 11 out of every 100 people in Sweden had been diagnosed with COVID-19. That number was 7.4 per 100 in Italy and 9.4 per 100 in the United Kingdom. Sweden also suffered ten times more deaths per capita than neighboring Norway.[14]

A NURSE'S PERSPECTIVE

Nanaz Fassih, a pediatric nurse in Sweden, did not agree with how Sweden's health officials decided to handle the pandemic. She tried wearing masks at work in hospitals and clinics, but she was told she wasn't allowed to. She lost her 83-year-old father to COVID-19 on Christmas Day, 2020. "I still believe in the government. I do," she said. "But I'm very, very sad about how they dealt with the issues with the pandemic."[15]

CHAPTER SIX

AFRICA

South Africa responded to the spread of COVID-19 with one of the world's earliest and strictest lockdowns. On March 5, 2020, a 38-year-old man tested positive for COVID-19. He had returned to South Africa from Italy. At the time, South Africa was one of only two countries in Africa that had reliable testing for COVID-19. With 3,000 people dead in Wuhan from COVID-19, South African president Cyril Ramaphosa felt the smartest thing the country could do was to close all borders and restrict movement.[1] On March 23, a three-week lockdown was imposed. There were 554 positive cases in the country.[2] The initial three-week lockdown stretched to six weeks.

Non-essential businesses were closed. People could leave their homes only to purchase groceries or for medical reasons. Socializing was forbidden, as were all outdoor activities, including sports. Dog owners were not allowed to walk their dogs outside.

South Africa's armed forces patrolled the streets during COVID-19 lockdowns.

President Ramaphosa deployed the army in the streets to make sure that people weren't leaving their homes. He set up a five-stage COVID-19 alert system to communicate how severe COVID-19 levels were.

HARDSHIPS FOR THE POOR

Middle-class South Africans were able to handle the lockdown well. Many were able to work from home with access to the internet. But impoverished communities struggled. A lack of food and financial resources led to looting and hunger riots. South Africa has a high percentage of unemployment. Many people rely on the welfare system to survive. Many others lost what little work they could find day to day during the lockdown. Furthermore, millions of South African school children get their daily food from their school meal programs. With schools closed, those children found themselves at home with no food. For these families, the threat of COVID-19 was soon coupled with the threat of starvation. The strict lockdowns made it very difficult for charitable organizations and relief societies to distribute food to those in need. Many criticized the government's lack of emergency planning for this situation.

Heading into the lockdown, testing sites were set up and hospitals were prepared. The South African health-care system was used to battling epidemics of HIV/AIDS and tuberculosis. Doctors and nurses were able to translate that experience to COVID-19. Few of South Africa's hospitals became overwhelmed. The country also experienced fewer deaths from the virus than predicted. South Africa, which ranks in the top three wealthiest countries in Africa, worked to communicate with and educate its people about COVID-19. With the country still in lockdown, it was able to

AN UNLIKELY TRUCE

One unexpected result of South Africa's strict lockdown was a temporary truce called by warring gangs that normally sell illegal drugs. Andie Steele-Smith, a pastor in Cape Town, received phone calls from leaders of two different gangs. They were hungry. "If these guys are starving, [and] they are at the top of the food-chain, the rest of the community is going to be in serious, serious strife," Steele-Smith said. He convinced rival gang members to come together to collect essential goods and distribute them throughout the communities struggling with hunger. "They're the best distributors in the country," he pointed out. Instead of distributing illegal drugs, the gang members began delivering food and necessities such as soap. "What we're seeing happen here is literally a miracle," Pastor Steele-Smith said.[3]

avoid overwhelmed hospitals through the first months of the pandemic.

The swift and strict lockdowns did slow the spread of COVID-19. But they were destroying the economy. In late April 2020, President Ramaphosa announced a plan to try to relieve some of the financial hardships caused by the pandemic.

By May 1, 2020, he began gradually decreasing the lockdown restrictions. Those continued to ease through September. But by January 2021, South Africa saw a surge of infections and a large uptick in COVID-related deaths. Throughout that month, the country averaged more than 500 deaths a day due to COVID-19. Things settled a bit in February, but by

INEQUALITY

Because of the lingering effects of apartheid, a system of segregation usually based on race that South Africa legally abolished in the 1990s, half of the nation still lives in poverty. Many black African adults do not live close to a clinic and don't have the means to travel to one. Though the government has tried to fix the effects of apartheid, South Africa is one of the most unequal countries in the world. Today, more than 70 percent of the country's wealth is owned by 1 percent of the population. Those living in poverty have few options when it comes to health care. For example, two-thirds of the ventilators in the country are in private clinics and hospitals, which many people simply cannot afford.[4]

June, and continuing throughout the summer into August, the number of deaths from COVID-19 averaged 300 to 400 a day.[5]

By January 2022, South Africa had experienced four waves of increased COVID-19 cases. During the fourth wave, scientists in the country identified a new variant of the virus called Omicron. This variant proved to be much more contagious than earlier variants. While the country had begun the pandemic with what seemed to be a good outlook, things turned throughout the course of a year and a half. South Africa entered 2022 with a tally of nearly 3.5 million COVID-19 infections since the beginning of the pandemic.[6] More than 91,000 South Africans had died from COVID-19, making it the worst-hit country in all of Africa, with an average of 152 deaths per 100,000 people.[7]

MALAWI

As news of COVID-19 spread in early 2020, officials in Malawi grew alarmed. Malawi is one of the poorest countries in the world. Maria Jose Torres, a United Nations (UN) worker in Malawi, reported, "Even a fairly low number of [COVID-19] cases could overwhelm the health system."[8] The first three cases of COVID-19 in Malawi were reported

Handwashing was an important preventive measure in Malawi.

on April 2, 2020, in Lilongwe. Five days later, another five cases were discovered and the first death in Malawi due to COVID-19 was reported. Malawian officials worked closely with support from UN agencies to slow the spread and prevent as many deaths as possible.

With the pandemic looming over their heads, many Malawians were dealing with another life-threatening problem. Flooding had destroyed much of the corn crop they relied on for food. The World Food Programme began a relief effort that included distributing cash to people at risk of starving. Cash distribution sites were also used as education areas where people could learn how to stay safe from COVID-19. Before receiving payments, recipients were told that staying a safe distance from each other and washing their hands helps prevent COVID-19.

Throughout 2020, the rate of COVID-19 infections in Malawi stayed relatively low. But in January 2021, the country experienced a surge of cases. A presidential home and a national stadium were turned into makeshift hospitals to treat severely ill COVID-19 patients. President Lazarus Chakwera declared a state of national disaster. "Our medical facilities are terribly understaffed, and our medical personnel are outnumbered," Chakwera said.[9] As cases climbed, more tent hospitals were set up on the front lawns of hospitals. President Chakwera gave weekly televised addresses on Sunday nights to keep Malawians updated on the situation. He also closed schools from mid-January to February 8, enforced nighttime curfews, and restricted gatherings to no more than 50 people.

COVID-19 vaccinations did not become available in Malawi until March 2021, three months later than in many wealthy countries, including the United States. President Chakwera and Vice President Saulos Chilima were the first Malawians to be vaccinated. Malawi struggled to vaccinate its people. Many people were hesitant to get the shot after hearing false information that it could lead to infertility. Additionally, many Malawians live in remote areas and were not able to travel to medical facilities to receive the shot. "When vaccines are available, we try as much as possible to make sure those in hard-to-reach areas are also targeted because if we don't make deliberate efforts to reach out to them, they often have to choose between using their money for transportation to a health facility or buying food for their families," explained Kedson Masiyano, a health center officer.[10] The Malawian government established an outreach program that allowed health-care workers to travel to rural areas to

Malawi faced challenges in rolling out COVID-19 vaccines.

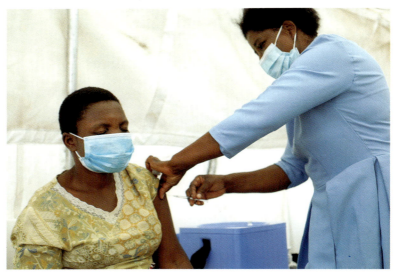

administer vaccines. By January 1, 2022 less than 4 percent of the eligible population was fully vaccinated.[11]

OTHER AFRICAN COUNTRIES

While the country of South Africa was hit hard, many other areas in Africa fared better. An outbreak of another deadly virus helped some areas of Africa better handle COVID-19. Since 1976, parts of Africa have dealt with outbreaks of Ebola virus disease, an infectious and often fatal disease that causes fever and severe internal bleeding. From 2014 to 2016, West Africa experienced the largest outbreak of Ebola since 1976. The outbreak killed more people than all other Ebola outbreaks combined, and it spread across Guinea, Sierra Leone, and Liberia. The Democratic Republic of the Congo also experienced an Ebola outbreak from 2018 to 2020. Health-care workers treating Ebola patients must take extreme precautions to protect themselves from becoming infected. This experience prepared them for dealing with the COVID-19 outbreak.

Countries neighboring those affected by the Ebola outbreak of 2014 to 2016, such as Côte d'Ivoire, Senegal, and Mali, had implemented screening for people crossing borders from the Ebola-stricken countries. These countries

REDUCING POACHING

Parts of Africa rely heavily on tourism, including countries such as Tanzania, which is famous for safari tours. But during the pandemic, safari tourism dwindled to nearly nothing. Many people could not fly to Africa because of flight restrictions. Additionally, travelers worried about being forced into lockdown or a quarantine in a foreign country if they tested positive or if there were a sudden outbreak. However, despite these challenges, some good came of this. Rhino poaching dropped dramatically in the first half of 2020. Poachers were unable to travel to or around Africa amid lockdowns and restrictions.

were able to include screening for COVID-19 as well. This helped to contain the spread of the virus. Additionally, these countries had mastered the practices of isolating infected people and contact tracing.

Other factors helped Africa fight the spread too. The population density in rural areas of Africa is low. This meant that social distancing was easier to achieve. In Nigeria, medical teams that had been traveling to villages to vaccinate children against polio were able to likewise educate these communities about the COVID-19 pandemic. Africa's strength was its community health systems.

However, there were significant challenges. The WHO established the goal of having at least 40 percent of people in every country vaccinated by the end of

December 2021. But just 9 percent of people in Africa were vaccinated by this deadline. Only seven African countries met the target. By the end of December, Nigeria had fully vaccinated only 2.1 percent of its citizens. The Democratic Republic of the Congo was at a meager 0.1 percent.[12] Lack of funding and training of medical staff, poor health infrastructure, and vaccine storage issues were all contributing factors. Some people were skeptical and fearful of getting vaccinated as well.

By January 2022, a total of 228,636 people had died in Africa. That's an average of 17 people per 100,000. By comparison, North America had 828,241 deaths, resulting in 249 deaths per 100,000.[13]

> "Vaccinating the whole world is the only way forward. Yet we continue to live with extreme vaccine discrimination, and Africa in particular is being left behind."[14]
>
> —Mo Ibrahim, chair of the Mo Ibrahim Foundation, which promotes the importance of governance and leadership for Africa

CHAPTER SEVEN

SOUTH AMERICA

Brazil prepared for COVID-19 by declaring it a public health emergency on February 3, 2020. Three days later, the Brazilian Ministry of Health approved a quarantine law. The law aimed at protecting the community by ensuring anyone testing positive for the virus would quarantine and those exposed would isolate.

The first-known COVID-19 case in Brazil was on February 25, 2020. The health department of São Paulo confirmed that a man returning from Italy had the virus. Shortly after, another person returning from Italy came down with COVID-19. Brazilian president Jair Bolsonaro advised the people of Brazil not to panic but to follow recommendations from the experts.

On March 12, Brazilian press secretary Fabio Wajngarten tested positive for COVID-19. He had recently accompanied President Bolsonaro to Miami, Florida, to meet with US president Donald

Jair Bolsonaro became president of Brazil in 2019.

Trump. Although Bolsonaro tested negative, within a few days, more members of the federal cabinet became ill. On March 19, Brazil closed its borders to neighboring countries. But COVID-19 was spreading among the people. By March 20, Brazil had almost 1,000 confirmed cases of COVID-19. On March 28, the Brazilian Ministry of Health reported there were 3,904 cases of COVID-19 in Brazil and 114 deaths.[1] Then, by April 10, the country counted its one thousandth death from COVID-19. The number of cases climbed to nearly 20,000. By April 30, Brazil's case count was beyond 87,000, surpassing China in the number of confirmed cases of COVID-19.[2]

Despite the fast spread of COVID-19 in Brazil, the president was eager to ease lockdowns that had been implemented the month before. Retail stores were allowed to open as long as face masks were worn. When Minister of Health Luiz Henrique Mandetta disagreed with Bolsonaro over social distancing guidelines, Bolsonaro fired him. From the beginning of the pandemic, doctors, disease experts, and world leaders have accused President Bolsonaro of minimizing the seriousness of COVID-19. While other countries were entering strict lockdowns, Bolsonaro argued against them, insisting they would destroy the Brazilian economy. In late 2020, when long-awaited vaccines were becoming available, he claimed he would not be getting one, voicing doubt about the safety of the vaccine shots. Speaking to the Brazilian public, he pointed out that in the Pfizer contract it was clear that the pharmaceutical company was not responsible for any side effects.

Brazilian military police officer Everaldo Pinto wore a Captain America costume while helping educate children about wearing masks and washing their hands.

RIO CANCELS CARNIVAL

Every year, the city of Rio de Janeiro observes the festive season of Carnival. Rio holds the largest Carnival celebration in the world, attracting millions of people who participate in partying. The week-long celebration takes place in late winter or early spring, just before the Christian period of Lent starts. The world-famous festival was canceled in 2021 to the disappointment of many. However, people were able to see online productions of teams who were well-known for their elaborate street performances. The venue typically used for Carnival celebrations was put to use as a vaccination spot. One singer popular at Carnival, Hildemar Diniz, sang as he went to get vaccinated.

Instead of backing vaccinations, the president chose to promote use of a COVID kit, which included medicines that had not been proven to work against COVID-19, such as hydroxychloroquine and ivermectin. Services such as YouTube and Facebook began to remove his posts and temporarily banned his accounts because they were spreading misinformation. In one video the president posted, he claimed there was a link between getting the vaccines and developing AIDS.

A year after the pandemic began, the global press labeled Brazil's handling of COVID-19 catastrophic. Many believed President Bolsonaro had mismanaged the pandemic in Brazil and that he and his advisers were to blame for the country's dire circumstances. In March 2021, Brazil's death toll due to COVID-19 stood at nearly 260,000.

Hospitals were near capacity, and only 3.8 percent of the population had been vaccinated.[3] By comparison, at that time, 15 percent of the US population had been vaccinated.[4] Brazil had to purchase one of the available vaccines from another country that was producing them. While other world leaders worked with vaccine companies to purchase doses, Brazil lagged with communication. Ilona Szabó de Carvalho, president of the public policy think tank Igarapé Institute, said, "Much of the blame for this nightmarish scenario lies at the feet of Bolsonaro and his circle of advisers. Rather than step up to address the issue, they have repeatedly played down the threat, ignored the advice of health experts and peddled conspiracy theories."[5]

In October 2021, a group of Brazilian

COVID-19 DEADLY TO BRAZIL'S CHILDREN

COVID-19 is rarely fatal for children, but Brazil had an unusually high number of deaths of children related to COVID-19. Between February 2020 and March 2021, 852 children younger than age nine had died because of COVID-19. Dr. Fatima Marinho, a doctor and researcher in Brazil, believed that these numbers represented less than half of the actual children who died of COVID-19, citing the lack of testing as the reason these deaths were underreported.[6] Experts say the number of child deaths in Brazil stemmed from the sheer number of cases of COVID-19.

senators voted to charge Bolsonaro with wrongdoing over his handling of the pandemic. A special senate investigative panel supported changes being filed for crimes against humanity. Although the president insisted he was not guilty, a representative from vaccine manufacturer Pfizer told the inquiry they repeatedly offered to sell vaccines to Brazil. Many emails were ignored. Yet, the number of COVID-related deaths hit more than 619,000, or 289 deaths per 100,000 people, at

Public transportation in Argentina had few riders during the lockdowns.

the end of December 2021.[7] Brazil had the second-highest number of deaths from COVID-19 in the world behind the United States.[8]

ARGENTINA

While Brazil's leaders took a relaxed approach to handling COVID-19, Argentina enforced much stricter guidelines. The country's first confirmed case was March 3, 2020. Four days later, the first death from COVID-19 in Argentina occurred. The patient was a 64-year-old man who had contracted the virus on a trip to Paris, France.

On March 19, Argentina went into a nationwide lockdown. It lasted until July and was one of the world's longest. During the

ARGENTINIAN CHILDREN IN LOCKDOWN

Lockdowns in the Argentinian capital of Buenos Aires lasted longer than those throughout the rest of the country. This was because of the population density of the city and the number of COVID-19 cases there. When lockdown restrictions were lifted a bit in Buenos Aires, children were allowed outside for the first time in 60 days. Children younger than age 16 could venture out for one hour on one day of the weekend. "Day after day they became anxious, and that was difficult," Veronica Corizzo explained of her two daughters who had been stuck in the house for two straight months. "Sixty days later, they are very happy to go out."[9]

lockdown, there were times when going outside to walk dogs or exercise was not allowed. Argentina's president Alberto Fernández closed the country's borders, and commercial flights into Argentina were banned for seven months. Schools and educational institutions were closed as well. Public gatherings were banned.

Although testing was slower to ramp up than in some neighboring countries, strict lockdowns helped to contain the spread of COVID-19 in Argentina. In May 2020, the country had just over 6,000 confirmed cases and 317 deaths. That same month, after seven weeks of lockdown, President Fernández allowed mayors and governors in Argentina's provinces to open up businesses if case numbers didn't start to climb. A poll that May showed 70.6 percent of Argentinians approved of how the government had handled the health crisis presented by the pandemic.[10]

"We are very happy to be one of the countries with a

> "I am aware that these restrictions create difficulties. Faced with this reality, there is no choice but to choose the preservation of life."[11]
>
> —Argentina's president Alberto Fernández

lower number of deaths," said Dr. Omar Sued, president of the Argentina Society of Infectious Diseases, in May 2020. Sued served as an adviser to President Fernández during the pandemic. He said officials realized early that if they didn't act, the country's health-care system would be overwhelmed. Without implementing lockdowns, predictions looked grim. "The first estimate said that we could have 250,000 deaths if we do nothing," he said.[12]

By January 2022, roughly 72 percent of Argentina's population had been fully vaccinated.[13] The number of infections since the beginning of the pandemic was 5.67 million.[14] The country had 117,181 deaths attributed to COVID-19, averaging 257 deaths per 100,000.[15]

WHAT IS COVAX?

Argentina was able to get a number of its vaccine doses through COVAX. The COVAX Facility is a global fund for vaccine development and procurement, led by the Coalition for Epidemic Preparedness Innovations, the Global Alliance for Vaccines and Immunization, the Pan American Health Organization, UNICEF, and the WHO. The coalition's goal is to guarantee the equitable distribution of COVID-19 vaccines worldwide. It has become the largest vaccine collection and supply operation in history. However, for a variety of reasons including supply issues and hesitancy, vaccine distribution was slow in poor countries into 2022.

CHAPTER EIGHT

NORTH AMERICA

Mexico confirmed its first case of COVID-19 on February 28, 2020. Two weeks later, on March 11, the WHO declared the COVID-19 outbreak to be a global pandemic. But Mexico's leaders did not enforce lockdowns, stay-at-home orders, or mask mandates. No travel restrictions were put in place. There was a lack of testing for those who were showing symptoms, so it was unclear exactly how many people were infected. The only direction the Mexican people received was to practice social distancing and good handwashing.

On March 15, Mexico City hosted a large music festival. The women's soccer championship games took place. Some people in Mexico, including state leaders, began to worry about the rise in cases of COVID-19. They wondered why the government had not taken steps to address the pandemic. Leaders in neighboring countries expressed frustration at the

On March 15, 2020, crowds of people gathered for the Vive Latino music festival in Mexico City, Mexico.

Mexican government's reluctance to take action. Some people noted that Mexico's president Andrés Manuel López Obrador wasn't practicing safe social distancing but instead was continuing to greet large groups of people at campaign rallies.

DRASTIC MEASURES

President Nayib Bukele of El Salvador took a stand against Mexico's lack of sanitary and safety measures by blocking a flight into his country from Mexico City on March 16. Bukele commented that Mexico did not have the ability to determine whether any of the plane's passengers had been infected. In comments on Twitter, President Bukele asked Mexico "to take drastic and overwhelming measures amid this pandemic." He went on to warn, "Otherwise, in 20 days the epicenter of this pandemic will not be Europe, but North America. Stop looking at this as something normal, please."[1]

As cases continued to climb, bars, nightclubs, movie theaters, and museums in Mexico City closed. On March 18, Mexico experienced its first COVID-related death. That same day, eight Mexican states closed their schools to slow the spread.[2] On March 19, Mexico's

Under Nayib Bukele's presidency, El Salvador took many measures to prevent the spread of COVID-19, including starting a lockdown on March 11, 2020.

General Health Council met. It made the decision to close all schools in Mexico. Within two weeks, the federal government suspended all nonessential activities. The Secretariat of Health launched the Healthy Distance program. It advised people throughout Mexico of the need for frequent handwashing and social distancing from others. But millions of households in Mexico do

SUSANA DISTANCIA AND THE HEALTH SQUAD

In an effort to communicate the need for social distancing and sanitary measures, Mexico's health ministry came up with a campaign using cartoon characters. The campaign was called Susana Distancia and the COVID-19 Health Squad. The campaign went viral. The heroine, Susana Distancia (*su sana distancia* translates to "your healthy distance") led a squad of four other cartoon heroines, each representing a stage in the Epidemiological Stoplight, a four-color monitoring system that let the people know when they could resume activities during the pandemic. Susana Distancia's sidekicks are Refugio (refuge), the red tier for staying home; Prudencia (prudence), the orange tier for avoiding going out; Esperanza (hope), the yellow tier for taking hygiene measures when going out; and Aurora, the green tier for the lowest risk, though people should still take precautions.

not have clean piped water, which makes handwashing difficult.

MEXICO BECOMES A HOT SPOT

Mexico's slow start to addressing the pandemic led to high rates of infection. By July 2020, Mexico was a hot spot for COVID-19 deaths, with about 28,000 people dead. Hospitals became overwhelmed. Crematoriums burned bodies around the clock. Desperate families took deceased loved ones out to the countryside for burial. By December, more than 106,000 Mexicans had died from the virus.[3] "What I saw was a total collapse of the health system," noted Francisco Moreno Sánchez, head of internal medicine at private medical institution Centro Médico ABC.[4]

In December 2020, good news was finally on the way. That month, Mexico became the first Latin American country to launch a vaccination program. Health-care workers began administering the Pfizer-BioNTech vaccine. It was hope for a country that had lost more than 120,000 people to the pandemic.[5]

Throughout 2021, Mexico continued to battle COVID-19. Unlike in other countries, Mexico's president did not push forward with a direct stimulus plan to give money to those who had lost jobs or were struggling financially because of the pandemic. People also found it difficult to get vaccines. In February 2021, India sent

> "You have to keep in mind that Mexico is facing this crisis with a very weak, understaffed, underequipped, health-care system. Now this means that flattening the curve will help, but the system will enter into an overload much faster than it has happened in other . . . countries."[6]
>
> —Eduardo Gonzalez-Pier, Mexican economist

doses of the AstraZeneca vaccine, and Belgium sent doses of the Pfizer-BioNTech vaccine. Instead of using these in areas of high population concentrations, like Mexico City, the president sent them to remote villages. Additionally, since the beginning of the pandemic, Mexico had not closed its borders to tourists and did not require them to show proof of negative test results to enter the country.

By the beginning of January 2022, only 56 percent of Mexico's population had been fully vaccinated.[7] The vaccination was not yet available to those 15 and younger. The country had lost almost 300,000 people to COVID-19, an average of 230 deaths per 100,000 people.[8] That was the fifth-highest death rate in the world.[9]

DISGUISED AND DESPERATE FOR VACCINES

When the COVID-19 vaccines first rolled out in Mexico, they were offered only to health-care workers, teachers, and people more than 60 years of age. However, two men in their thirties dyed their hair and eyebrows white to appear older in order to receive a vaccine earlier than they should have. They showed up at a vaccination center in Mexico City with fake IDs and wearing masks and face shields. After receiving their shots, their true age came to light when the men spoke to workers at the facility. Their voices sounded much younger than 60. They were both arrested and investigated in conjunction with their fake IDs.

CANADA

Canada's approach to the pandemic was much stricter than Mexico's. At the onset, Canada closed its borders. The only people allowed in were Americans who lived close to the border and crossed into Canada daily for work or Americans who had to drive through Canada to reach Alaska.

Canada's geography gave it a natural advantage over the United States and Mexico throughout the pandemic. Canada has a larger land mass than the United States but less than one-ninth the population. Two-thirds of Canadians live within 62 miles (100 km) of the US border, but Canada does not have cities as densely populated as New York City, for example.[10] People are spaced out farther in Canada than in the United States.

Canada confirmed its first case of COVID-19 on January 23, 2020, within a week of the United States' first confirmed case. But Canada's COVID-19 health crisis did not explode like it did for its neighbors to the south. By July, the United States had three times the number of COVID-19 cases per capita compared with Canada and nearly twice the number of deaths.[11]

MAKING MUSIC IN LOCKDOWN

On March 22, 2020, members of the Toronto Symphony Orchestra came together virtually to perform for Canadians in lockdown. The orchestra's principal double bass player, Jeffrey Beecher, arranged for players to record themselves playing their own parts of a piece of music. He then edited all the videos together to create a virtual performance of the last movement from Aaron Copland's *Appalachian Spring*. The music was written in 1942 while the world was battling in World War II. "The intent was to offer something of solace," Beecher explained of the unique video performance.[12]

READY TO GO

In the early stages of the pandemic, Canada was successful in setting up testing sites, which enabled it to isolate the sick, trace contacts, and limit the spread of the disease. Canada's leading hospitals were prepared for the increase of patients COVID-19 would create. Although health-care workers were initially worried about a lack of PPE such as hospital-grade masks and gowns, the country was able to quickly increase production of those items. Canadian provinces established face mask mandates, requiring people to use masks while indoors.

On March 11, Canadian prime minister Justin Trudeau announced a relief fund of $1 billion in Canadian dollars ($728 million in US dollars). Half of the funds would go to provinces and territories, $50 million was for the WHO, and $275 million was to be spent on COVID-19 research

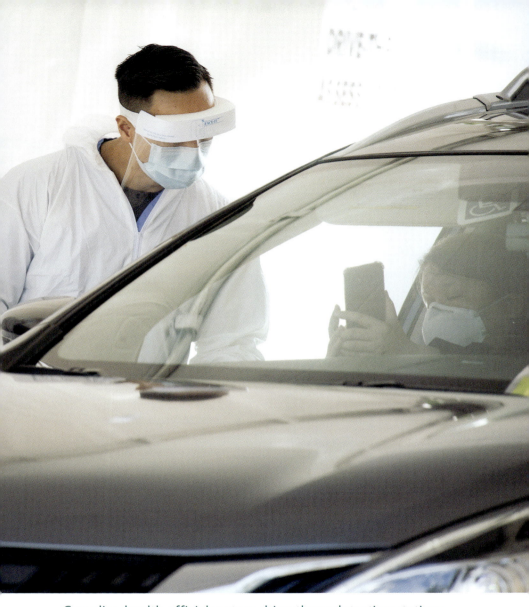

Canadian health officials set up drive-through testing stations in early 2020.

in Canada.[13] By July, Canadian residents who had lost their jobs were eligible to apply for direct monthly payments distributed for four months.

Throughout 2020, cases in Canada and the rest of the world began to surge. In November, Prime Minister Trudeau urged people to stay home. Projections had indicated cases could hit 20,000 per day by the end of December. Trudeau allowed leaders in each province to decide how to manage lockdowns for their residents. Lockdown measures were widely followed by Canadians, and political parties typically worked together instead of against each other. Provinces shared excess PPE gear with other provinces facing greater need.

A NEW SHOE FOR A NEW HERO

Dr. Bonnie Henry, the provincial health officer of British Columbia, became a spokesperson to the Canadian people. They found her regular televised updates to be informative and comforting. She reminded people to be good to each other in the face of the pandemic. "This is our time to be kind, to be calm and to be safe" was her trademark line.[14] When famous Vancouver shoemaker John Fluevog found out Henry wore his shoes on some of her broadcasts, he decided to create a special design in her honor. The shoes, two-tone pink leather Mary Jane heels, were a hit. Fluevog's company planned to make a limited number of the shoes, but there was such a demand for the heels that it had to make more. Henry's words "be kind, be calm, be safe" were featured on the shoes. Part of the sales from the Dr. Henry shoes went to support the WHO's COVID-19 Response Fund.

VACCINATIONS ROLL OUT

COVID-19 vaccines were made available to Canadians in December 2020. By the beginning of January 2022, 77 percent had been fully vaccinated.[15] Although more than 30,000 Canadians had died of COVID-19 by the end of 2021, an average of 80 deaths per 100,000, Canada was faring better than many other countries around the globe.[16] In August 2021, after more than a year of closed

Canadians lined up to get vaccinated at vaccine clinics, some of which were in stadiums.

97

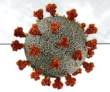

COVID-19 BY THE NUMBERS

MORTALITY BY COUNTRY[17]

Some countries were more successful than others in slowing the spread of COVID-19 and keeping the total number of deaths relatively low. Different factors greatly affected each country's ability to slow the virus's spread, such as population density, health-care system preparedness, lockdown procedures, geography, and more. Each country had its own approach. The graph shows the number of deaths for every 100,000 people due to COVID-19 in the countries mentioned in the book through February 28, 2022. At this time, the global death rate from the disease was 76 per 100,000 people.[18]

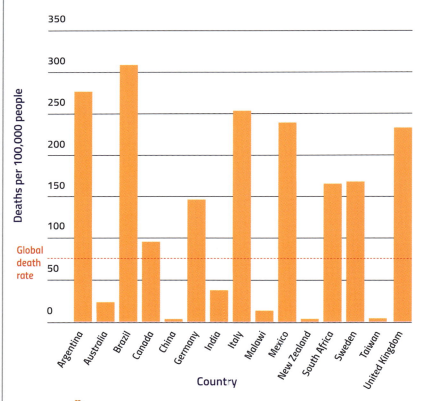

98

borders, Canada opened to fully vaccinated Americans for non-essential travel.

Throughout the course of the COVID-19 pandemic, every country around the world had to decide how to handle the crisis within its own borders. Many lessons were learned along the way, and those lessons will likely be incorporated into planning and preparations for future pandemics. Throughout the first few years of battling COVID-19, one thing became very clear: handling a pandemic is not something that happens only within a country's borders. Viruses do not recognize borders. Handling a global pandemic takes everyone, in every country, working toward reducing the spread of the disease.

ESSENTIAL FACTS

KEY EVENTS
- The first case of what would become known as COVID-19 is reported in Wuhan, China, in December 2019.
- On January 30, 2020, the WHO declares COVID-19 a global health emergency.
- On March 5, 2020, a 38-year-old man in South Africa tests positive for COVID-19.
- Italy's prime minister Giuseppe Conte announces on March 9, 2020, that Italy will be entering a strict lockdown to slow the spread of COVID-19.
- By March 20, 2020, the Australian government has banned all travelers coming into Australia who are not residents returning home from abroad.
- In December 2020, COVID-19 vaccinations begin to roll out in a number of countries.
- Sweden decides to not mandate lockdowns. By August 2021, the nation has recorded more cases of COVID-19 per capita than most other countries.

KEY PEOPLE
- Italy's prime minister Giuseppe Conte enacted a very strict lockdown in Italy after struggling with overrun hospitals and a high death count.
- German chancellor Angela Merkel spoke to the German people via television, telling them the situation was serious. She then closed schools, restaurants, and shops.
- South African president Cyril Ramaphosa closed borders and restricted movement by imposing a three-week lockdown beginning March 23, 2020.

- Brazilian president Jair Bolsonaro made global headlines when he decided to avoid lockdowns and criticized health experts. Brazil's number of people infected with COVID-19 skyrocketed.
- Jacinda Ardern, New Zealand's prime minister, took quick action, closing the nation's borders for the first time in history and banning large gatherings, leading to a relatively low number of COVID-19 cases in New Zealand early on.

KEY STATISTICS

- Within weeks after the first confirmed case, COVID-19 had spread to every continent except Antarctica.
- By the end of April 2021, India had recorded a total of 200,000 COVID-related deaths. By late May, the country hit 300,000 deaths, bringing the per capita rate to 21.8 deaths per 100,000 people.
- By 2022, more than 5.4 million people around the world had died from COVID-19, approximately 69 deaths for every 100,000 people.
- Mexico had lost more than 300,000 people to COVID-19 by January 2022, an average of 230 deaths per 100,000 people, the fifth-highest death rate in the world.

QUOTE

"I think that we'll remember the shock we felt in the first week of March for a very long time: the people taking to supermarkets in a panic, the hardships of the most vulnerable. But we'll also remember the strength ordinary people had to react."

—Stefano Marrone, a volunteer in Milan, Italy

GLOSSARY

antibody
A protein that the immune system uses to fight infection.

antigen
A substance that does not naturally occur in the body and that causes the body's immune system to attack it.

conspiracy theory
A belief, without proof, that an individual or a group is responsible for an event or crime.

crematorium
A furnace for burning bodies or a building containing such a furnace.

epicenter
During the COVID-19 pandemic, an area with the most cases and spread of disease.

infrastructure
A system of buildings, equipment, and staff.

lockdown
Time during COVID-19 when most businesses, schools, and more were closed and most travel was restricted to help control the spread of the virus.

mandate
An official order to do something.

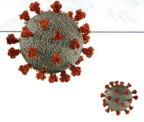

personal protective equipment (PPE)
Supplies such as surgical masks, rubber gloves, and gowns that help prevent infection and are most often used by medical personnel.

province
A division of a country, similar to a state.

relief package
Money issued by the government to put toward paying unemployment benefits, individual stimulus checks, and grants to small businesses and individuals to help during an economic downturn.

stimulus
Something that prompts further activity.

variant
A strain of a virus that may contain one or more mutations.

ventilator
A machine that helps a patient breathe when the lungs don't function properly for any reason.

welfare
Government programs that assist people in financial need.

ADDITIONAL RESOURCES

SELECTED BIBLIOGRAPHY

Allam, Zaheer. "The First 50 Days of COVID-19: A Detailed Chronological Timeline and Extensive Review of Literature Documenting the Pandemic." *NCBI*, 24 July 2020, ncbi.nlm.nih.gov. Accessed 25 Jan. 2022.

"Coronavirus Disease (COVID-19)." *WHO*, 2022, who.int. Accessed 1 Jan. 2022.

"COVID-19 Dashboard: Global Map." *Johns Hopkins University of Medicine*, 2022, coronavirus.jhu.edu. Accessed 1 Jan. 2022.

FURTHER READINGS

Allen, John. *The Origins and Spread of COVID-19*. ReferencePoint, 2021.

Idzikowski, Lisa, ed. *The Politics and Science of COVID-19*. Greenhaven, 2022.

Mooney, Carla. *COVID-19 Vaccines and Treatments*. Abdo, 2023.

ONLINE RESOURCES

To learn more about fighting COVID-19 abroad, please visit **abdobooklinks.com** or scan this QR code. These links are routinely monitored and updated to provide the most current information available.

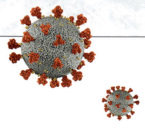

MORE INFORMATION

For more information on this subject, contact or visit the following organizations:

GLOBAL ALLIANCE FOR VACCINES AND IMMUNIZATION (GAVI)

2099 Pennsylvania Ave. NW, Suite 200
Washington, DC 20006
202-478-1050
gavi.org

Gavi is an organization with headquarters in the United States and Switzerland. It works to keep people healthy around the world by increasing access to vaccines. It was one of the organizations leading COVAX, through which some countries received their COVID-19 vaccines.

PAN AMERICAN HEALTH ORGANIZATION (PAHO)

525 23rd St. NW
Washington, DC 20037
202-974-3000
paho.org

The Pan American Health Organization is the WHO's headquarters in the Americas. The WHO is an organization that helps protect global health. It is responsible for declaring pandemics, and it provided nations with guidance for how to respond during the COVID-19 pandemic.

105

SOURCE NOTES

CHAPTER 1. ITALY
1. Vanessa Romo and Sylvia Poggioli. "Italy Expands Quarantine Measures Nationwide." *NPR*, 9 Mar. 2020, npr.org. Accessed 6 Apr. 2022.
2. "Coronavirus: Italy." *Worldometer*, 6 Apr. 2022, worldometers.info. Accessed 6 Apr. 2022.
3. Erica Firpo. "Italy's Inspiring Response to the Coronavirus." *BBC Travel*, 26 Mar. 2020, bbc.com. Accessed 6 Apr. 2022.
4. Denise Chow and Emmanuelle Saliba. "Italy Has a World-Class Health System. The Coronavirus Has Pushed It to the Breaking Point." *NBC News*, 19 Mar. 2020, nbcnews.com. Accessed 6 Apr. 2022.
5. Hannah Ritchie et al. "Coronavirus (COVID-19) Cases." *Our World in Data*, 6 Apr. 2022, ourworldindata.org. Accessed 6 Apr. 2022.
6. Hannah Ritchie et al. "Coronavirus (COVID-19) Deaths." *Our World in Data*, 7 Apr. 2022, ourworldindata.org. Accessed 7 Apr. 2022.
7. Alessio Perrone. "'The Strength of Ordinary People.' The Creative Ways Italians Are Supporting Each Other during Their Coronavirus Lockdown." *Time*, 7 Apr. 2020, time.com. Accessed 7 Apr. 2022.
8. Ritchie et al., "Coronavirus (COVID-19) Cases."
9. "1918 Pandemic (H1N1 virus)." *CDC*, n.d., cdc.gov. Accessed 7 Apr. 2022.
10. Nicholas LePan. "Visualizing the History of Pandemics." *Visual Capitalist*, 14 Mar. 2020, visualcapitalist.com. Accessed 7 Apr. 2022.
11. "The Black Death: The Plague, 1331–1770." *John Martin Rare Book Room*, 2017, hosted.lib.uiowa.edu. Accessed 7 Apr. 2022.
12. Ritchie et al., "Coronavirus (COVID-19) Deaths."

CHAPTER 2. CHINA
1. Zaheer Allam. "The First 50 Days of COVID-19: A Detailed Chronological Timeline and Extensive Review of Literature Documenting the Pandemic." *Surveying the COVID-19 Pandemic and Its Implications*, 2020, pp. 1–7, ncbi.nlm.nih.gov. Accessed 7 Apr. 2022.
2. Allam, "The First 50 Days of COVID-19."
3. "Li Wenliang: Coronavirus Kills Chinese Whistleblower Doctor." *BBC News*, 7 Feb. 2020, bbc.com. Accessed 7 Apr. 2022.
4. Lily Kuo. "Coronavirus: Panic and Anger in Wuhan as China Orders City into Lockdown." *Guardian*, 23 Jan. 2020, theguardian.com. Accessed 7 Apr. 2022.
5. Guo Jing. Interview with Grace Tsoi. "Coronavirus Wuhan Diary: Living Alone in a City Gone Quiet." *BBC News*, 30 Jan. 2020, bbc.com. Accessed 7 Apr. 2022.
6. Paulina Cachero. "Wuhan Residents on Coronavirus Lockdown Are Facing Food Shortages." *Insider*, 2 Mar. 2020, businessinsider.com. Accessed 7 Apr. 2022.
7. Kim Hjelmgaard, Eric J. Lyman, and Deirdre Shesgreen. "This Is What China Did to Beat Coronavirus. Experts Say America Couldn't Handle It." *USA Today*, 1 Apr. 2020, usatoday.com. Accessed 7 Apr. 2022.
8. Adam Jeffery. "Coronavirus: Photos of Wuhan after 11-Week Lockdown." *CNBC*, 8 Apr. 2020, cnbc.com. Accessed 7 Apr. 2022.
9. Farah Master and Joyce Zhou. "Hong Kong, World's Most Visited City, Faces Tourism Bust." *Reuters*, 19 Nov. 2020, reuters.com. Accessed 7 Apr. 2022.

CHAPTER 3. ASIA
1. Hannah Ritchie et al. "Taiwan: Coronavirus Pandemic Country Profile." *Our World in Data*, 7 Apr. 2022, ourworldindata.org. Accessed 7 Apr. 2022.
2. Keoni Everington. "Taiwan Deploys Chemical Warfare Troops to Disinfect Taoyuan." *Taiwan News*, 21 Jan. 2021, taiwannews.com.tw. Accessed 7 Apr. 2022.
3. Hannah Ritchie et al. "Coronavirus (COVID-19) Vaccinations." *Our World in Data*, 7 Apr. 2022, ourworldindata.org. Accessed 7 Apr. 2022.
4. Udani Samarasekera. "India Grapples with Second Wave of COVID-19." *The Lancet Microbe*, vol. 2, no. 6, June 2021, p. E238, thelancet.com. Accessed 7 Apr. 2022.
5. Samarasekera, "India Grapples with Second Wave."

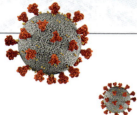

6. Alasdair Pal, Rupam Jain, Sumit Khanna, and Rajendra Jadhav. "Mass Cremations, Day and Night." *Reuters Graphics*, 28 May 2021, graphics.reuters.com. Accessed 7 Apr. 2022.

7. Hannah Ritchie et al. "Coronavirus (COVID-19) Deaths." *Our World in Data*, 7 Apr. 2022, ourworldindata.org. Accessed 7 Apr. 2022.

8. Ritchie et al., "Coronavirus (COVID-19) Vaccinations."

9. Sophia Ankel. "The COVID-19 Death Toll in India Could Be up to 10 Times Higher Than the Official 200,000 Figure, Experts Say." *Insider*, 1 May 2021, businessinsider.com. Accessed 7 Apr. 2022.

CHAPTER 4. AUSTRALIA AND NEW ZEALAND

1. Anika Stobart and Stephen Duckett. "Australia's Response to COVID-19." *Health Economics, Policy, and Law*, vol. 17, no. 1, 2022, pp. 95–106, ncbi.nlm.nih.gov. Accessed 7 Apr. 2022.

2. Renju Jose. "Australia's Worst-Hit State Says COVID-19 Hospitalisations May Plateau Next Week." *Reuters*, 13 Jan. 2022, reuters.com. Accessed 7 Apr. 2022.

3. Stobart and Duckett, "Australia's Response to COVID-19."

4. Nick Baker. "How Australia Went from Being a 'COVID-Free Paradise' to 'A Mess.'" *NBC News*, 23 Aug. 2021, nbcnews.com. Accessed 7 Apr. 2022.

5. Shane Wright. "Cost of Lockdowns Is $17 Billion and Counting." *Sydney Morning Herald*, 13 Aug. 2021, smh.com.au. Accessed 7 Apr. 2022.

6. Renju Jose. "Melbourne Readies to Exit World's Longest COVID-19 Lockdown." *Reuters*, 20 Oct. 2021, reuters.com. Accessed 7 Apr. 2022.

7. "Coronavirus (COVID-19) at a Glance—31 December 2021." *Australian Government Department of Health*, 31 Dec. 2021, health.gov.au. Accessed 7 Apr. 2022.

8. Hannah Ritchie et al. "Coronavirus (COVID-19) Deaths." *Our World in Data*, 7 Apr. 2022, ourworldindata.org. Accessed 7 Apr. 2022.

9. Susan Strongman, Michael Hall, Michelle Cooke, and Rose Davis. "Timeline: The Year of COVID-19 in New Zealand." *RNZ*, 24 Mar. 2021, rnz.co.nz. Accessed 7 Apr. 2022.

10. Strongman et al., "Timeline: The Year of COVID-19 in New Zealand."

11. Madeleine Chapman. "How Did New Zealand Take On COVID-19, and Win?" *Black Inc.*, n.d., blackincbooks.com.au. Accessed 7 Apr. 2022.

12. Strongman et al., "Timeline: The Year of COVID-19 in New Zealand."

13. Hannah Ritchie et al. "Coronavirus (COVID-19) Vaccinations." *Our World in Data*, 7 Apr. 2022, ourworldindata.org. Accessed 7 Apr. 2022.

14. Ritchie et al., "Coronavirus (COVID-19) Deaths."

15. "Criticism Grows over New Zealand's COVID-19 Vaccine Rollout to Maori Community." *SBS News*, 19 Oct. 2021, sbs.com.au. Accessed 7 Apr. 2022.

CHAPTER 5. EUROPE

1. Ralf Bosen and Jens Thurau. "COVID: How Germany Battles the Pandemic—A Chronology." *DW*, 28 Dec. 2021, dw.com. Accessed 7 Apr. 2022.

2. Melissa Eddy. "Flare-Up in Virus Cases Sets Back Germany's Efforts to Reopen." *New York Times*, 25 June 2020, nytimes.com. Accessed 7 Apr. 2022.

3. Associated Press. "Germany's COVID Timeline: From First Case to 100,000 Dead." *ABC News*, 25 Nov. 2021, abcnews.go.com. Accessed 7 Apr. 2022.

4. Hannah Ritchie et al. "Coronavirus (COVID-19) Vaccinations." *Our World in Data*, 7 Apr. 2022, ourworldindata.org. Accessed 7 Apr. 2022.

5. "Coronavirus: Germany to Go into Lockdown over Christmas." *BBC News*, 13 Dec. 2020, bbc.com. Accessed 7 Apr. 2022.

6. Geir Moulson. "Germany to Toughen Restaurant Rules, Cut COVID Quarantine." *ABC News*, 7 Jan. 2022, abcnews.go.com. Accessed 7 Apr. 2022.

7. "The Wiesn 2020 Cannot Take Place Because of COVID-19." *Oktoberfest.de*, 21 Apr. 2020, oktoberfest.de. Accessed 7 Apr. 2022.

8. Lydia McMullan, Pamela Duncan, Garry Blight, Pablo Gutiérrez, and Frank Hulley-Jones. "COVID Chaos: How the UK Handled the Coronavirus Crisis." *Guardian*, 3 Feb. 2021, theguardian.com. Accessed 7 Apr. 2022.

9. McMullan et al., "COVID Chaos."

10. Ritchie et al., "Coronavirus (COVID-19) Vaccinations."

SOURCE NOTES CONTINUED

11. Hannah Ritchie et al. "Coronavirus (COVID-19) Deaths." *Our World in Data*, 7 Apr. 2022, ourworldindata.org. Accessed 7 Apr. 2022.

12. Aria Bendix. "A Year and a Half after Sweden Decided Not to Lock Down, Its COVID-19 Death Rate Is up to 10 Times Higher Than Its Neighbors." *Insider*, 21 Aug. 2021, businessinsider.com. Accessed 7 Apr. 2022.

13. Bendix, "A Year and a Half after Sweden Decided Not to Lock Down."

14. Bendix, "A Year and a Half after Sweden Decided Not to Lock Down."

15. Mallory Pickett. "Sweden's Pandemic Experiment." *New Yorker*, 6 Apr. 2021, newyorker.com. Accessed 7 Apr. 2022.

CHAPTER 6. AFRICA

1. David McKenzie and Bukola Adebayo. "South Africa Records Its First Case of Coronavirus." *CNN*, 5 Mar. 2020, cnn.com. Accessed 7 Apr. 2022.

2. Nancy Stiegler and Jean-Pierre Bouchard. "South Africa: Challenges and Successes of the COVID-19 Lockdown." *Annales Medico-Psychologiques*, vol. 178, no. 7, 2020, pp. 695–698, ncbi.nlm.nih.gov. Accessed 7 Apr. 2022.

3. "'Literally a Miracle': Violent Rival Gangs in South Africa Call Truce to Help People During Pandemic." *CBS News*, 18 Apr. 2020, cbsnews.com. Accessed 7 Apr. 2022.

4. Jason Beaubien. "The Country with the World's Worst Inequality Is." *NPR*, 2 Apr. 2018, npr.org. Accessed 7 Apr. 2022.

5. Hannah Ritchie et al. "Coronavirus (COVID-19) Deaths." *Our World in Data*, 7 Apr. 2022, ourworldindata.org. Accessed 7 Apr. 2022.

6. Hannah Ritchie et al. "Coronavirus (COVID-19) Cases." *Our World in Data*, 7 Apr. 2022, ourworldindata.org. Accessed 7 Apr. 2022.

7. Ritchie et al., "Coronavirus (COVID-19) Deaths."

8. RCO Malawi. "Malawi Braces for COVID-19." *United Nations COVID-19 Response*, n.d., un.org. Accessed 7 Apr. 2022.

9. "Malawi Setting Up Field Hospitals to Cope with Virus Surge." *VOA*, 3 Feb. 2021, voanews.com. Accessed 7 Apr. 2022.

10. "Rolling Out COVID-19 Vaccines in Malawi amid Hesitancy and Supply Challenges." *World Bank*, 19 Oct. 2021, worldbank.org. Accessed 7 Apr. 2022.

11. Hannah Ritchie et al. "Coronavirus (COVID-19) Vaccinations." *Our World in Data*, 7 Apr. 2022, ourworldindata.org. Accessed 7 Apr. 2022.

12. Peter Mwai. "Covid-19 Vaccinations: African Nations Miss WHO Target." *BBC News*, 31 Dec. 2021, bbc.com. Accessed 7 Apr. 2022.

13. Ritchie et al., "Coronavirus (COVID-19) Deaths."

14. Tommy Wilkes. "'Extreme' Vaccine Discrimination Risks Leaving Africa Behind—Report." *Reuters*, 5 Dec. 2021, reuters.com. Accessed 7 Apr. 2022.

CHAPTER 7. SOUTH AMERICA

1. Márcia Rodrigues and Plínio Aguiar. "Brasil Tem 114 Mortes e 3.904 Casos Confirmados de Coronavírus [Brazil Has 114 Deaths and 3,904 Confirmed Cases of Coronavirus]." *R7*, 28 Mar. 2020, noticias.r7.com. Accessed 7 Apr. 2022.

2. "COVID-19 Map." *Johns Hopkins Coronavirus Resource Center*, 7 Apr. 2022, coronavirus.jhu.edu. Accessed 7 Apr. 2022.

3. Ilona Szabó de Carvalho. "Brazil's Handling of COVID-19 Is a Global Emergency." *Americas Quarterly*, 3 Mar. 2021, americasquarterly.org. Accessed 7 Apr. 2022.

4. Cecelia Smith-Schoenwalder. "CDC: 15% of US Population Fully Vaccinated against Coronavirus." *US News & World Report*, 29 Mar. 2021, usnews.com. Accessed 7 Apr. 2022.

5. Szabó de Carvalho, "Brazil's Handling of COVID-19."

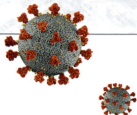

6. Nathalia Passarinho and Luis Barrucho. "Why Are So Many Babies Dying of COVID-19 in Brazil?" *BBC News*, 15 Apr. 2021, bbc.com. Accessed 7 Apr. 2022.

7. Hannah Ritchie et al. "Coronavirus (COVID-19) Deaths." *Our World in Data*, 7 Apr. 2022, ourworldindata.org. Accessed 7 Apr. 2022.

8. "Number of Novel Coronavirus (COVID-19) Deaths Worldwide as of April 4, 2022, by Country." *Statista*, Apr. 2022, statista.com. Accessed 7 Apr. 2022.

9. "COVID-19: Argentina Children Allowed Outdoors." *YouTube*, uploaded by CGTN America, 17 May 2020, youtube.com. Accessed 7 Apr. 2022.

10. Philip Reeves. "Argentina Reacted Early and Kept the Coronavirus Largely Contained." *NPR*, 12 May 2020, npr.org. Accessed 7 Apr. 2022.

11. "COVID: Argentina Starts New Lockdown as Cases Soar." *BBC News*, 22 May 2021, bbc.com. Accessed 7 Apr. 2022.

12. Reeves, "Argentina Reacted Early."

13. Hannah Ritchie et al. "Coronavirus (COVID-19) Vaccinations." *Our World in Data*, 7 Apr. 2022, ourworldindata.org. Accessed 7 Apr. 2022.

14. Hannah Ritchie et al. "Coronavirus (COVID-19) Cases." *Our World in Data*, 7 Apr. 2022, ourworldindata.org. Accessed 7 Apr. 2022.

15. Ritchie et al., "Coronavirus (COVID-19) Deaths."

CHAPTER 8. NORTH AMERICA

1. Rafael Bernal. "Mexico under International Criticism for Coronavirus Response." *The Hill*, 18 Mar. 2020, thehill.com. Accessed 7 Apr. 2022.

2. "Mexico's Response to COVID-19: A Case Study." *UCSF Institute for Global Health Sciences*, n.d., globalhealthsciences.ucsf.edu. Accessed 7 Apr. 2022.

3. Hannah Ritchie et al. "Coronavirus (COVID-19) Deaths." *Our World in Data*, 7 Apr. 2022, ourworldindata.org. Accessed 7 Apr. 2022.

4. Nacha Cattan and Vernon Silver. "How Mexico Forgot Its COVID Crisis." *Bloomberg*, 15 July 2021, bloomberg.com. Accessed 7 Apr. 2022.

5. Ritchie et al., "Coronavirus (COVID-19) Deaths."

6. "Ground Truth Briefing | Evaluating the Impact of COVID-19 in Mexico." *Wilson Center*, 26 Mar. 2020, wilsoncenter.org. Accessed 7 Apr. 2022.

7. Hannah Ritchie et al. "Coronavirus (COVID-19) Vaccinations." *Our World in Data*, 7 Apr. 2022, ourworldindata.org. Accessed 7 Apr. 2022.

8. Ritchie et al., "Coronavirus (COVID-19) Deaths."

9. "Mexico Likely to Surpass 300K COVID-19 Deaths This Week, Fifth Highest Worldwide." *NBC News*, 6 Jan. 2022, nbcnews.com. Accessed 7 Apr. 2022.

10. Amanda Coletta. "Canada's Coronavirus Performance Hasn't Been Perfect. But It's Done Far Better Than the US." *Washington Post*, 15 July 2020, washingtonpost.com. Accessed 7 Apr. 2022.

11. Coletta, "Canada's Coronavirus Performance."

12. Brad Wheeler. "Toronto Symphony Orchestra Brings Aaron Copland's *Appalachian Spring* to Life." *Globe and Mail*, 24 Mar. 2020, theglobeandmail.com. Accessed 7 Apr. 2022.

13. Amanda Connolly. "Trudeau Announces $1B Coronavirus Response Fund for Provinces, Territories." *Global News*, 11 Mar. 2020, globalnews.ca. Accessed 7 Apr. 2022.

14. Christina Farr. "How Canada Is Fighting COVID-19: Ramping Up PPE Production, Travel Ban from the US and Bonnie Henry." *CNBC*, 15 July 2020, cnbc.com. Accessed 7 Apr. 2022.

15. Ritchie et al., "Coronavirus (COVID-19) Vaccinations."

16. Ritchie et al., "Coronavirus (COVID-19) Deaths."

17. Ritchie et al., "Coronavirus (COVID-19) Deaths."

18. "COVID-19 Coronavirus Pandemic." *Worldometer*, 7 Apr. 2022, worldometers.info. Accessed 7 Apr. 2022.

INDEX

Antarctica, 12, 13
antibodies, 33, 55, 57
apartheid, 68
apps, 25, 26, 55
Ardern, Jacinda, 47–48
Argentina, 83–85, 98
Australia, 39–45, 98
   Melbourne, 39, 41, 43

Bolsonaro, Jair, 77–78, 80–82
borders, 6, 14, 27, 29, 40–41, 47, 51, 65, 73, 78, 84, 92–93, 99
Brazil, 77–83, 98
Bukele, Nayib, 88

Canada, 93–99
Carnival, 80
Centers for Disease Control and Prevention, US, 33
Chakwera, Lazarus, 71
children, 7–8, 12, 14, 66, 74, 81, 83
China, 12, 19–27, 39, 78, 98
   Hong Kong, 27
   Wuhan, 11, 19–27, 30, 33, 65
Christmas, 55–56, 63

contact tracing, 30, 50, 55, 59–60, 74, 94
Conte, Giuseppe, 6–7, 11
COVAX, 85
COVID-19 Health Squad, 90
crematoriums, 11, 36, 37, 90
cruise ships, 46

deaths, 15–17, 75
   Argentina, 84–85, 98
   Australia, 45, 98
   Brazil, 78, 80, 81, 82–83, 98
   Canada, 93, 97, 98
   China, 22, 98
   Germany, 53, 55, 98
   India, 35, 36–37, 98
   Italy, 5, 7, 11, 14, 98
   Malawi, 70, 98
   Mexico, 88, 90, 92, 98
   New Zealand, 51, 98
   South Africa, 67–69, 98
   Sweden, 62–63, 98
   Taiwan, 30, 98
   United Kingdom, 58, 60, 98

Democratic Republic of the Congo, 73, 75

El Salvador, 88

Fassih, Nanaz, 63
Fernández, Alberto, 84–85

Germany, 53–57, 98
   Bavaria, 53, 54, 57
Guo Jing, 25

Hanson, Claudia, 63
Henry, Bonnie, 96
herd immunity, 57–58, 61–62
HIV/AIDS, 16, 67, 80
hospitals, 9–11, 14, 21, 22, 25, 35, 54, 58, 63, 67–68, 71, 81, 90, 94
   Charité, 54
   Taoyuan General Hospital, 31

India, 32–37, 91, 98
Italy, 5–15, 39, 53–54, 63, 65, 77, 98
   Rome, 7–8

job loss, 33–34, 91, 95
Johnson, Boris, 58

110

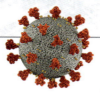

Li Wenliang, 22
lockdowns, 7, 12, 14, 24, 27, 33, 36, 40–44, 46, 48, 50, 54–55, 60, 62, 65–68, 74, 78, 83–85, 87, 94, 96, 98
López Obrador, Andrés Manuel, 88, 91
Lunar New Year, 23, 32

mail, 42
Malawi, 69–73, 98
Māori people, 51
masks, 11, 14, 25–26, 30–31, 41, 51, 54, 59–60, 62, 63, 78, 87, 92, 94
Merkel, Angela, 53, 55–56
Mexico, 87–93, 98
    Mexico City, 87–88, 92
Morrison, Scott, 40

New Zealand, 36, 45–51, 98
    Auckland, 47–48, 50
Nigeria, 74–75

1918 influenza pandemic, 15, 16, 41

oxygen, 35

personal protective equipment (PPE), 11, 58, 94, 96
Pfizer, 49–50, 79, 82, 91–92
poaching, 74

quarantine, 8, 15, 20, 22, 24, 26, 29–30, 39, 43, 50, 55–56, 74, 77

Ramaphosa, Cyril, 65–66, 68

schools, 5–6, 12, 14, 29, 40, 46, 48, 55, 58, 62, 66, 71, 84, 88–89
South Africa, 65–69, 73, 98
Steele-Smith, Andie, 67
Sued, Omar, 85
Sweden, 60–63, 98
symptoms, 6, 17, 19, 22, 26, 30, 54, 87

Taiwan, 29–32, 98
Tegnell, Anders, 62
Test and Trace, 59–60
testing, 12, 13, 14, 30, 32, 35, 39, 50, 54–55, 58–60, 65, 67, 74, 77–78, 81, 84, 87, 92, 94
Toronto Symphony Orchestra, 94
Trudeau, Justin, 94, 96

United Kingdom, 36, 57–60, 63, 98
University of Bonn, 54

vaccines, 13–14, 15, 17, 32, 33, 37, 42–45, 49–51, 56–57, 60–62, 71–75, 79–82, 85, 91–92, 97–99
variants, 17, 33, 43, 50, 56, 69

World Food Programme, 70
World Health Organization (WHO), 12, 19, 33, 74, 85, 87, 94, 96

111

ABOUT THE AUTHOR

SUSAN E. HAMEN

Susan E. Hamen lives in Minnesota with her husband, Ryan, and her son and daughter. Hamen is the author of more than 30 books for children. Some of her favorite topics have included World War II, ancient Rome, and what the world was like before online shopping and social media. She has spent nearly two years working exclusively from home due to the COVID-19 pandemic, trading the company and conversations of her coworkers for the daily companionship of the family's two cats. Hamen and her family have had fun coming up with creative ways to take family trips while maintaining social distancing. She looks forward to the day when COVID-19 is no longer an imminent threat to people.

ABOUT THE CONSULTANT

JUDD L. WALSON, MD, MPH

Dr. Judd L. Walson is vice chair of the Department of Global Health and a professor of Global Health, Medicine (Infectious Disease), Pediatrics and Epidemiology at the University of Washington. Dr. Walson completed his training in both internal medicine and pediatrics residencies at Duke University, had a fellowship in infectious disease at the University of Washington, and holds a master's degree in public health from Tufts University. Dr. Walson has experience in the design and implementation of large clinical trials in resource-limited settings. Dr. Walson has worked at the WHO. He is particularly interested in interventions targeting vulnerable children to improve childhood survival, cognitive development, and growth.